The Cultural and Social Foundations of Education

Series Editor
A. G. Rud
College of Education
Washington State University
Pullman, WA, USA

D1593385

The Palgrave Pivot series on the Cultural and Social Foundations of Education seeks to understand educational practices around the world through the interpretive lenses provided by the disciplines of philosophy, history, sociology, politics, and cultural studies. This series focuses on the following major themes: democracy and social justice, ethics, sustainability education, technology, and the imagination. It publishes the best current thinking on those topics, as well as reconsideration of historical figures and major thinkers in education.

More information about this series at
http://www.palgrave.com/gp/series/14443

Kerry T. Burch

Jefferson's Revolutionary Theory and the Reconstruction of Educational Purpose

palgrave
macmillan

Kerry T. Burch
College of Education
Northern Illinois University
DeKalb, IL, USA

The Cultural and Social Foundations of Education
ISBN 978-3-030-45765-5   ISBN 978-3-030-45763-1   (eBook)
https://doi.org/10.1007/978-3-030-45763-1

Cover illustration: © nadia/E+/gettyimages

This Palgrave Macmillan imprint is published by the registered company Springer Nature
Switzerland AG
The registered company address is: Gewerbestrasse 11, 6330 Cham, Switzerland

ACKNOWLEDGMENTS

It is a humbling experience to write a book about Jefferson. In writing it, I have constantly been reminded of my debt to scores of Jefferson scholars both past and present. Had I not been able to stand on their collective shoulders, this book could not have been written. Two authors in particular played a decisive role in helping me form the main idea of the book. First, my encounter with Michael Hardt's small volume on Jefferson as a "revolutionary" figure came as a big surprise, leading me to take Jefferson's revolutionary credentials far more seriously than I previously had. Not long after coming across Hardt's book, I read Danielle Allen's *Our Declaration*, a magisterial work that offered a stunning treatment of how the essential principles of the Declaration of Independence could be applied to contemporary circumstances. Without the combined influence of these two authors, the idea for this book would not have come into focus. I would also like to acknowledge the crucial and timely support that Northern Illinois University provided to this project in the form of a sabbatical leave in 2016. My students at NIU also helped me enormously by asking probing questions about the Jeffersonian themes that I've taught over the past few years. Without their collective influence, it's would be hard to imagine how the book would get formed much less completed. Many thanks are also due to the entire team at Palgrave Macmillan. I refer specifically to the editor of *The Cultural and Social Foundations of Education* Series, A. G. Rud, to the education editor, Milana Vernikova, and to assistant editor, Linda Braus. I was also fortunate enough to have benefited from two anonymous reviewers whose suggestions and overall critique, no doubt, made the book stronger than it would have been otherwise. I will remain forever grateful to all of these fine professionals for their stewardship of the production process. Finally, on a more personal note, I'd like to express my appreciation for the enthusiastic support of my immediate and extended family: to my radical sister, Shelley, who showed me what resistance meant very early on, to my nieces, Sonali and Juliana who teach in Chicago and the Chicago area, to my nephew Jayme, a top-notch union organizer in Chicago, and to Dash and Coco, the latest editions to the family; also, to dear friends of mine who have lived with my Jeffersonian preoccupations over the last few years, especially Sarah, Tim, Cara, Fluff, Molly, and Jess. Thank you all!

CONTENTS

CHAPTER 1

Introduction

The generation which commences a revolution can rarely complete it.
—Thomas Jefferson, 1823

Today we routinely hear Americans declare that the republic is in a state of existential crisis. In news media, commentators opine that even the most finely wrought descriptive words cannot begin to capture the enormity of the crisis. The emergence of the COVID-19 pandemic, moreover, has greatly magnified these related crises. For purposes of clarification, then, it may be useful to frame the problems of the moment as paradigmatic in nature, as a system-wide crisis consisting of a set of concomitant, interconnected crises. Crises over the status of truth in public discourse; crises over corporate corruption in a post-*Citizens United* world; crises over the country's unconstitutional forever wars; crises over a seemingly irreversible planetary ecocide led by the United States; crises over a neoliberal educational regime whose defining feature appears to be the civic and democratic demoralization of America's public schools; and finally, crises over a combined sense of hopelessness and what might be called outrage fatigue. A rapid intensification of these political and cultural contradictions seems to be the hallmark of our era.[1]

---

[1] The paradigmatic analysis here is indebted to many authors, below I name a few. Thomas S. Kuhn's *The Structure of Scientific Revolutions*. Chicago: University of Chicago Press, 1996 helps us to map structural transformations in many arenas. Kuhn's insight that

© The Author(s) 2020
K. T. Burch, *Jefferson's Revolutionary Theory and the Reconstruction of Educational Purpose*, The Cultural and Social Foundations of Education, https://doi.org/10.1007/978-3-030-45763-1_1

On the educational front, teacher strikes in Arizona, West Virginia, Kentucky, Oklahoma, Colorado, North Carolina, and in the city of Chicago, among other locales, speak at once to the shameful conditions that teachers face and to the hope that their underlying causes may soon be addressed. From a paradigmatic standpoint, it seems as if the very purposes of education that neoliberalism has imposed upon the nation's schools in the last few decades itself constitutes one of our deepest systemic problems and challenges. Since the public schools have always been in the business of modeling some form of identity or another, as they necessarily must, the question arises: As possible models of human identity toward which the schools might aspire to educate the young, should they continue along the path charted by neoliberalism and concern themselves primarily with reproducing versions of *Homo Economicus*? Or, should the schools recover their civic purposes and concern themselves primarily with reproducing versions of *Homo Civicus*?[2]

This book is an invitation to think through these questions and problems from a Jeffersonian perspective. It makes the case that a critical engagement with the most radical dimensions of Jefferson's educational philosophy—what I am calling his revolutionary theory—can establish a

---

paradigm shifts historically have occurred when "anomalies" and "contradictions" begin to accumulate within any given explanatory model/paradigm, suggests that we are presently on the cusp of such a transformational shift. For a much needed account of how the American warfare state is destroying the very conditions that make democracy possible, see Tom Engelhardt's *A Nation Unmade by War*. Chicago: Haymarket Books, 2018. My analysis is also indebted to David Blacker's *What's Left of the World: Education, Identity and the Post-Work Political Imagination*. London: Zero Press, 2019. Blacker's assessment of our educational future is bleak, and I think this reinforces the need for paradigmatic rather than incremental change. For an incisive look at the dismal state of civic education today, see Michael Rebell's *Flunking Democracy: Schools, Courts and Civic Participation*. Chicago: University of Chicago Press, 2018. As both an education litigator and professor at Teachers College, Columbia University, Rebell effectively gives the United States an "F" when it comes to providing a decent civic education to the nation's youth. For a powerful and poetic reflection on the irreversibility of climate warming and its consequences, see David Wallace-Wells's, *The Uninhabitable Earth: Life After Warming*. New York: Tim Duggan Books, 2019.

[2] It is common for authors in various disciplines to employ the trope of "Homo Economicus/Homo Civicus" as a way to theorize how the ongoing tensions between capitalist and democratic moral imperatives are manifest within individuals in educational and other social spheres. One of the best discussions of this trope, including the destructive effects of neoliberalism on education today, can be found in Wendy Brown's, *Undoing the Demos: Neoliberalism's Stealth Revolution*. Brooklyn: Zone Books, 2015.

rational basis upon which to reestablish both the civic purposes of public education and the quality of our democracy. I believe that the educational challenges posed by the predicaments outlined above can be most intelligently met—and remedied—when interpreted in relation to the democratic-revolutionary tradition launched by the American Revolution. I further contend that if teachers in particular were to develop a keener appreciation for what is most "revolutionary" about the American Revolution, it would not only illuminate many contemporary predicaments, but its remembrance could serve as a resource for envisioning and working toward a more just and democratic America. In this regard, I am increasingly convinced that however well-intentioned our efforts on behalf of educational reform, they are bound to fail to the degree they are symbolically and normatively *untethered* from the nation's democratic-revolutionary tradition. We turn to Jefferson today to re-tether ourselves to this forgotten tradition.[3]

Perhaps the most cogent expression of the radical democratic tradition of the American Revolution is Thomas Jefferson's revolutionary theory.[4] In the following chapters, the goal is to articulate how a better grasp of Jefferson's revolutionary vision can serve as a kind of moral and pedagogical compass for both restoring and redirecting the democratic civic purposes of public education.

In broad conceptual strokes, the idea of permanent revolution signifies a positive cultural orientation to conflict and to political renewal.[5] Whatever terminology we use, whether "revolutionary theory" or theory of "permanent revolution," the theory's defining quality for Jefferson was both processual and moral (*moral* because it contained a democratic telos,

---

[3] For a trenchant and wide-ranging account of Jefferson's overlooked radical side, see Richard Matthews, *The Radical Politics of Thomas Jefferson: A Revisionist View*. Lawrence, KS: University of Kansas Press 1986.

[4] The conceptual validity of this claim is rooted in the following three sources. More recently, Michael Hardt, in his *Thomas Jefferson: The Declaration of Independence*. London: Verso, 2007, makes a strong case for validating Jefferson's revolutionary credentials. Tellingly, Hardt's book is part of a series by Verso Books on revolutionary thinkers. I was surprised to see Jefferson included in such a series, alongside books on the revolutionary thought of Mao, Ho Chi Minh, Gramsci, Robespierre, Guevara, Lenin, Zizek, and others. Dan Sisson's, *The Revolution of 1800: How Jefferson Rescued Democracy from Tyranny and Faction—And What It Means Today*. San Francisco: Berrett-Koehler, 2013, affirms Jefferson's claim that the election of 1800 should indeed be properly framed as a revolution. Hannah Arendt's *On Revolution*, New York: Penguin Classics, 1963, is widely recognized to have fortified Jefferson's status as a revolutionary thinker.

[5] Hardt, see "Thomas Jefferson, Or, The Transition of Democracy," vii–xxv.

or end-in-view). The theory can be posited interchangeably as a revision-ary state of being, a conceptual framework, a discourse, and importantly, as a form of democratic rhetoric. This rhetorical dimension is crucial to bear in mind, for Jefferson deployed the theory rhetorically to serve as a conduit for channeling the mythopoetic Spirit of 76.[6] The function of the theory as a form of rhetoric was not to describe the static and finished dimensions of reality (to the extent any exist), but rather to theorize his-torical reality in all of its kaleidoscopic permutations.

Because of the democratic and inter-generational teleological founda-tion of Jefferson's revolutionary theory, it aptly symbolizes that which is most revolutionary about the American Revolution.[7] The "most revolu-tionary" quality of the nation's founding event did not rest, for example, on the fact that the American patriots successfully seized state power from the British. The most revolutionary dimension of the American Revolu-tion was the idea that its success would depend on its moral values being enacted and reenacted, generation after generation.[8] Jefferson repeatedly observed that the ultimate success, or vindication, of the American Rev-olution would hinge on whether subsequent generations of Americans would have the capacity and willingness to re-imbue the meaning of the Spirit of 76 into novel historical circumstances, unforeseeable circum-stances that would require politically and culturally inventive efforts to refresh the meaning of its core values.[9]

The ultimate status of the American Revolution, then, would depend on the ability of the American people to learn the art of revising the mean-ing of that Spirit as new conditions and new needs developed over suc-cessive generations. According to this historiographic perspective, it was not the formal structures of US government (e.g., checks and balances,

[6] I use the term "mythopoetic" as a designator for the Spirit of 76 because I think it captures its mythological and poetic character (note: the etymology of *poiesis* (Gr.) means "to create"). For more on the meaning of *poiesis,* see Jim Garrison, *Dewey and Eros: Wisdom and Desire in the Art of Teaching.* New York: Teachers College Press, 1997, xv, 8–9, 24, 49, 71, 88.

[7] In Greek, *telos* means "end," thus, in this context, teleological refers to the ultimate purpose of Jefferson's theory: that being, the perpetual transition toward deeper levels of democratization.

[8] Hardt, "Transition and Democracy," xv–xxi.

[9] For a concise formulation of this Jeffersonian principle, consult Annette-Gordon Reed's and Peter Onuf's magisterial, *"Most Blessed of the Patriarchs": Thomas Jefferson and the Empire of the Imagination.* New York: W. W. Norton & Company, 2016, 235. It is worth noting that the "Spirit of 76" is indexed ten times, a measure of its centrality to Jefferson's thought.

election cycles) that was most significant about the American Revolution, as important as they were. As suggested, what was most revolutionary was the historical emergence of a Spirit & Idea, a secularized religious project that gave birth to the nation's democratic-revolutionary tradition. This mythical terrain, as a meaning narrative, represented a sharp discontinuity from ancient regimes and their monarchies, standing armies and entrenched aristocratic elites. Yet, we could also trace the discursive lineage of this spirit to ancient democratic Athens, to the classical republican tradition, and to the radical democratic strand of the Enlightenment tradition.[10] For Jefferson, this new animating spirit seemed to contain a "mythopoetic" quality, a moral geography, if you will, capable of summoning up within individual's emotional intensities and devotions to a set of democratic moral ideals. In the chapters ahead, I make the case that Jefferson's discourse of permanent revolution can be interpreted as a hermeneutic through which the symbolic field of meanings sequestered within the Spirit of 76 can be channeled and empirically realized.[11]

Unfortunately, however, the popular image of the American Revolution that most of us pick up along the way is rooted in an assumption that the revolution was, above all, a finite event synonymous with, and reducible to, the military phase of the conflict (1775–1782). Jefferson's revolutionary theory explicitly rejects this mechanical conception of the founding. His theory assumes instead that our revolution should not, ultimately, be imagined as something finished or complete, but should rather be imagined as a perpetually unfinished historical project. In other words, the popular image of the American Revolution taught in the schools tends to conflate and confuse a finite war with a set of inter-generationally embodied moral purposes. One of the essential features of Jefferson's revolutionary thought is that it highlights the significance of this conceptual distinction.

Turning to the curricular implications of Jefferson's revolutionary theory, I argue that its defining elements point directly to the importance of developing in students' their capacities to revise, to improvise, to experiment, to rebel, to remember, and to become mindful of political

[10] For a comprehensive intellectual history of the American Revolution, republican ideology, and its enlightenment-informed emergence, see Jonathan Israel, *The Expanding Blaze: How the American Revolution Ignited the World, 1775–1848*. Princeton: Princeton University Press, 2017.

[11] Philosopher Richard Bernstein has recently brought his analytical acumen to the American Revolution in his *Why Read Hannah Arendt Now*. London: Polity, 2018. See, "The American Revolution and the Revolutionary Spirit," 103–116.

ambition and greed in all its guises. A Jeffersonian-inspired redirect of curricular purpose today, would certainly mean, among other things, a restoration of the centrality of both civic education and the humanities into the K-12 curriculum. Jefferson valued these traditions because he understood that the foundational pillars of a republican civic identity—freedom, truth, reason, civic engagement, to name a few—were moral capacities whose development depended in no small measure on the tradition of the humanities. Although Jefferson was not the only founder to link the survival of the republic to the project of educating the intelligence and virtue of the American people, he was perhaps the most eloquent in establishing the crucial linkages between education and the ongoing nature of the revolution. It is on these moral and curricular grounds, that I recruit Jefferson today as an iconic, if controversial resource for providing insight into the ongoing task of educating virtuous democratic citizens and societies.

In writing the book, I am mindful that, for some readers, Jefferson's racist pronouncements and practices may well nullify any prospect that his theories could have contemporary relevance. It is not my intention in this book to condemn or to praise Jefferson so much as it is to grasp what he was trying to "get at" in formulating his revolutionary thought. Rather than ignoring the growing number of critical perspectives on the slave-holding enlightener from Monticello, I frame Jefferson as a synecdoche of the nation, as a figure who continues to stand for and symbolize the ideals, contradictions, hopes, and tragedies gyrating at the nucleus of American political culture.[12] As many authors before me have observed, to inquire into Jefferson, is also to inquire into the often baffling, contradictory, ambiguous, and tragic qualities of the American experience itself. An examination of these problematic facets of Jefferson's life reveals some stark reminders. First, we must recognize the danger of uncritically appropriating the thought of any eighteenth-century figure for purposes of interpreting twenty-first century conditions. Perhaps more importantly, we should never overlook Jefferson's most egregious shortcoming: His failure, despite his democratic sympathies, to promote a multi-racial image of national identity for America's future.[13]

---

[12] Peter Onuf/Jan Lewis, "American Synedoche: Thomas Jefferson, as Image, Icon, Character and Self." In *The Mind of Thomas Jefferson*, ed. Peter Onuf. Charlottesville: University of Virginia Press, 2012, 85–94.

[13] Reed/Onuf, *Blessed are the Patriarchs*, Preface, 11–25. This work is groundbreaking in large part because the authors, while unflinching in their criticisms of Jefferson, are also

THE STYLE AND STRUCTURE OF THE BOOK

The book has been influenced by the style of writing adopted by two giants in my disciplinary field: John Dewey and George Counts. As chief architects of the twin disciplines of philosophy of education and the social foundations of education, Dewey and Counts frequently deployed a genre of writing that combined a critical analysis of American power relations with a healthy dose of philosophical reflection. Dewey biographer Alan Ryan, for example, describes many of his essays as "lay sermons."[14] This book seeks to extend that tradition. Ryan defines the lay sermon as a genre of writing located at the intersection where philosophical analysis meets the advocacy of new public policies, and where professional academics, through their writing, initiate meaningful conversations about current affairs with the broader reading public. Without engaging in conceptual overreach, I believe that, in important respects, the lay sermon can be regarded as a form of rhetoric that bears strong, albeit secular, resemblances to the American jeremiad tradition. It is for this and other reasons, explained below, that the book is organized according to the jeremiad's three-part thematic structure. I adopt this format because the telos, or end-in-view, of Jefferson's revolutionary theory recapitulates, in both substance and form, this uniquely American form of rhetoric.

As Sacvan Bercovitch, David Murphy, David Howard-Pitney, and George Shulman have articulated, all types of jeremiadic texts—from the speeches of Jonathan Edwards and Frederick Douglass to Eugene Debs and Martin Luther King—partake of the same thematic structure, despite other differences in moral and ideological substance.[15] The structure of the Puritan rhetorical trope unfolds in three sequences. In the first

cognizant of his pedagogical value as an object of study. It's not about elevating Jefferson or tearing him down, rather his value lies in understanding his contested role throughout American history in the formation of national identity.

[14] See Alan Ryan, *John Dewey and the High Tide of American Liberalism*. New York: W. W. Norton & Company, 1995, 265–266.

[15] Although the literature is vast on the jeremiad style of rhetoric, my own understanding of it is particularly indebted to the following authors: Sacvan Bercovitch *The American Jeremiad*. Madison: University of Wisconsin Press, 1986; Andrew R. Murphy, *Prodigal Nation: Moral Decline and Divine Punishment: From New England to 9/11*. Oxford: Oxford University Press, 2011; David-Howard-Pitney, *African-American Jeremiad: Appeals to Justice in America*. Philadelphia: Temple University Press, 2005; George Shulman, *American Prophecy: Race and Redemption in American Political Culture*. Minneapolis: University of Minnesota Press 2018.

sequence, the speaker or writer reminds their audience about the rich significance and promise of their agreed-upon social covenant. In the second sequence—the declension—the speaker excoriates congregants for having so deplorably lost sight of their founding vision. Here, the "chosen people" risk botching their lovely experiment unless prophetically called back to renew the values of their original vision. In the third sequence, the audience is offered a redeeming vision of renewal in which their moral devolution can be turned around, but only if a new connection is forged with the forgotten values that once defined their community.

In the context of this book, then, the "promise" is the secular promise of Jefferson's democratic-friendly revolutionary theory, upon whose creative execution the fulfillment of the revolution depends. The "declension" element comes into play in the chapters ahead as we realize the extent to which the character of today's politics, education, and culture has turned nakedly oligarchic, thereby posing an existential threat to the nation's democratic experiment. As to the future-oriented "renewal" phase, I argue that renewal may come when and if the American people can learn, metaphorically, to pour the old vintage wine of Jefferson's revolutionary theory into newly refashioned, twenty-first century bottles. As our title suggests, this means that Americans will be successful today in reconstructing the purposes of education beyond the parameters of neoliberalism, to the degree that we can recover the moral impulses that animated Jefferson's educational vision.[16]

There is another tradition related to the jeremiad that also colors the book's approach. Here I am referring to the democratic strand of the American political tradition. I write as a philosopher of education indebted to the traditions of Socratic and Freirean pedagogy, but also to the democratic strands of the American political tradition. In several chapters, for example, I link Jefferson's animus against standing armies to figures like George Washington, Dwight Eisenhower, and Martin Luther King, Jr., who reflected similar beliefs in their writings. In other chapters, I argue for a recovery of the relevance and meaning of the Declaration of Independence through an examination of Abraham Lincoln's prophetic

---

[16]While Jefferson's educational vision was limited in important ways, as will be discussed in Chapter 3, I maintain that it's still useful today in the sense that it underscores the fundamental civic purposes of education, and it is precisely this quality that requires recovery in our times.

writings on the Declaration. In other chapters, I situate Jefferson's educational and revolutionary thought alongside the work of John Dewey and George Counts. Thus, I write within the American political tradition, a tradition that I believe still retains a great deal of potential power to transform things for the better, provided, of course, that we reframe these strands in the right way. Among other things, then, the book is an attempt to recover the radical democratic potential of the nation's rich but all too often neglected political tradition.

What makes the book particularly distinctive, then, is that it does not stop after providing an in-depth examination of Jefferson's revolutionary theory in its eighteenth- and early nineteenth-century contexts. It proceeds beyond this and seeks to apply the insights afforded by Jefferson's theory to the contemporary and future educational scene. No other Jefferson title that I am aware of today occupies this past, present, and future space. Owing to the fact that Jefferson's revolutionary theory contains a strong future-directed trajectory, I believe that it would lose much of its potential transformative power if we were to conceptualize it in isolation from the present and future.

Part I, Promise, covers Chapters 2 through 5. The first chapter defines the essential features of Jefferson's theory. The second chapter discusses its' educational implications and how they might be articulated and mined theoretically for their contemporary significance. In Chapters 4 and 5, I examine the ways in which two influential educational theorists of the twentieth century, John Dewey and George Counts, respectively, provided critical updates to Jefferson's revolutionary thought in the midst of the Great Depression.

Part II, Declension, consists of Chapters 6 through 8. These chapters are anchored in constitutional amendments that Jefferson proposed but were never enacted (namely, no standing armies, freedom from monopolies, and a federal education amendment). The core aim of Part II is to describe, on the one hand, why the failure to enact these three constitutional amendments symbolizes a form of democratic moral declension and, on the other, how the critical spirit underlying each of the proposals can be reignited in classrooms today.

The chapters in Part II are organized in three sections. The first sections establish the historical context of the proposed amendments and discuss the ways in which they fit into and augment Jefferson's theory of permanent revolution. The second sections highlight the so-called declension element, that is, how the moral principles and values of the amendments have been virtually eclipsed and overwhelmed by contemporary empirical realities. The third sections of each chapter are renewal-oriented and theoretically experimental, in that they consider how the moral spirit undergirding the respective amendments might be imaginatively retrieved today, both as a means for analyzing the present and for rejuvenating our democratic political imaginations.

Part III, Renewal, consists of Chapters 9 through 11. In this thematic sequence, I begin by restating in capsule form what I take to be the defining revisionary features of Jefferson's theory. The normative aims and future-directed character of the concluding chapters represent an homage to Jefferson's desire for bringing about revolutionary change through the reconstruction of educational purpose. In a contemporary update to Jefferson's spirit of curricular innovation and experimentation, I maintain that the best way for the public schools to meet the evolving needs of American youth would be for them to implement a Jeffersonian-inspired reconstruction of educational purpose. What is most needed, I contend, is for the schools to "re-found" their fundamental purposes to better align themselves with that which is most revolutionary about the American Revolution. This final section of the book tells a story about what it would mean to recover these values and to embark upon a journey of moral renewal along several fronts: educationally, politically, and culturally.

PART I

Promise: Revolutionary Rhetoric for a Democratic America

CHAPTER 2

What Is Jefferson's Revolutionary Theory?

CHARTING THE CONTOURS OF THE DISCOURSE

Jefferson's theory of permanent revolution can be understood as a loosely knit yet generalizable set of propositions intended to drive home the idea that the American Revolution—for it to fulfill itself—must be understood in multi-generational terms. At the broadest level, then, the theory's core aim involves a rejection of framing the American Revolution as a onetime, finite event, as if it were something coterminous with the military phase of the conflict with England (1776–1782). In contrast to this popularly accepted imaginary, leading figures of the American Revolution, notably Jefferson, John Adams, and Benjamin Rush, insisted that the revolution should be seen, above all, as an ongoing process of cultural and political transformation.[1]

The theory finds expression mainly through Jefferson's voluminous private correspondence. Nowhere does Jefferson provide a tidy systematic approach for understanding any of his philosophical, political, and educational writings. He never refers explicitly to his "theory of permanent revolution," nor does he have any titles or books on the subject where further conceptual precision might be developed. This absence in

---

[1] See David Tyack, "Forming the National Character: Paradox in the Educational Thought of the Revolutionary Generation." *Harvard Educational Review*, Vol. 36, No. 1, 29–41.

© The Author(s) 2020
K. T. Burch, *Jefferson's Revolutionary Theory and the Reconstruction of Educational Purpose*, The Cultural and Social Foundations of Education, https://doi.org/10.1007/978-3-030-45763-1_2

Jefferson's approach, however, should not be regarded as a limitation to the chapter's aim of mapping the normative aims and conceptual boundaries of the concept. Rather, we can benefit from Jefferson's revolutionary theory when we view it foremost as a form of democratic rhetoric. While Jefferson never undertakes a systematic effort to clarify the premises of the concept, he still manages to explain its general meaning in a morally cogent and evocative literary fashion.

In what follows, I select passages from Jefferson's letters that, in various ways, highlight his attempts to furnish a language to describe a set of intertwined moral, political, and educational visions for interpreting the radical flux of social and historical transformation. Jefferson seemed to believe that only if the American people regarded the revolution as something deeply processual would they be able to keep regenerating the nation's democratic cultural life. Jefferson's letter-writing campaigns, undertaken over a period of half a century, makes available a substantial amount of primary text from which we can begin to chart the outlines of the moral, democratic, and educational principles underlying his revolutionary theory.

The first expressions of Jefferson's idea of permanent revolution are found in the Declaration of Independence. It is implicit in the document's preamble, residing within the clause that grants the "Right of the People to alter or to abolish" any government that betrays the consent of the people and thus becomes "destructive" of those ends— human rights, public happiness—that defined its ostensible purpose. Jefferson adds that if the People have determined that the conditions for legitimate rebellion have been met, "it is the right, it is the duty to throw off such government," and to institute new forms of government "most likely to effect their Safety and Happiness."[2]

In boldly codifying the Right of the People to alter or abolish their government as one of the nation's defining moral principles, Jefferson and the Continental Congress simultaneously elevated to a position of privilege another related moral principle—the right to dissent. The right to dissent is intertwined with Jefferson's framework of permanent revolution in several ways. First, and most obviously, it's indivisibly linked to the right to freedom of speech, as individual speech acts can embody acts of dissent. In addition, Jefferson saw in this constitutional principle a legal and

---

[2] Pauline Maier (ed.), *The Declaration of Independence and the Constitution of the United States.* New York: Bantam Books, 2008, p. 53.

political mechanism that would open up imaginative cultural spaces for reordering the American mindscape. The right to revolution, free speech, and dissent, can thus be seen as allied vehicles of inter-generational social transformation. If the Declaration elevated the right to revolution to a privileged place within the nascent political culture, the Constitutions' amendment process elevated this same principle, albeit in a very limited way according to Jefferson, who remarked that the requirements for revising the Constitution through the amendment process were too onerous.[3]

As one constitutional scholar informs us, the right to revolution, or the right to "Alter and Abolish" governments, are clauses that found formal expression in most state constitutions in the decades after 1776.[4] Arguably, the integration of the right to revolution into most of the state's new constitutions, coupled with its prior integration into the Declaration and US Constitution, suggests that, at the nation's inception, the right to revolution assumed the status of a common sense idea within the public imagination.

For the larger purposes of the book, it is essential to point out that democratic theorist Sheldon Wolin offers a less state-centric, more explicitly cultural-centered interpretation of the right to revolution. Wolin has articulated that the meaning of the right really boils down to "the right to create new forms."[5] In other words, Wolin expands the conventional boundaries of the clause to emphasize that the right embraces not only the right to create new *governmental* forms when necessary, but the right to create new *cultural* forms when necessary. This conceptual expansion is crucial. Among other things, it means that attempts to spark social change, to engage in various acts of peaceful revolution—that is, to create new cultural forms—are practical activities that should be understood as so many acts of political creativity. Although Jefferson may not have written explicitly about the distinction between legal and cultural forms of revolutionary action, his educational proposals, under review in

---

[3] Thomas Jefferson to Adamantios Coray, October 31, 1823.

[4] See Christian G. Fritz, *American Sovereigns: The People and America's Constitutional Tradition Before the Civil War.* Cambridge: Cambridge University Press, 2008, 24–25.

[5] Sheldon Wolin, "What Revolutionary Action Means Today." In *Dimensions of Radical Democracy: Pluralism, Citizenship, Community,* ed. Chantal Mouffe. London: Verso, 1992, 249.

Chapter 3, can be understood to implicitly serve the purpose of bring-ing into being novel cultural forms of civic identity.[6] These new forms of civic identity, moreover, were envisioned to play a vital role in tran-sitioning the American republic toward deeper levels of democratization. For this reason, Jefferson would have likely concurred with Wolin that the right to revolution is a right that can and should find expression in both the legal and cultural arenas. Indeed, the same sentiment was expressed by Benjamin Rush in 1786, when he declared that the American Revolution was "not over," arguing that it wasn't over because it had yet to effect a change in the American people's principles, opinions, and manners so as to fit the new governmental form.

Wolin's expansion of the clause's meaning underscores the fact that ongoing transitions toward democracy invariably rely on prior transfor-mations in the cultural sphere as a precondition for transformations in the state sphere. A brief review of the historical record suggests, for example, that a conceptual continuity threads through the abolitionist, suffragette, and twentieth-century civil rights movements. Despite some obvious dif-ferences between these social movements, they share a commonality inso-far as they were all framed by official authorities as dangerous renegade political bodies acting outside the boundaries of the constitution and state. And while each of these dissent-driven social movements began their reform projects as tiny minorities acting within the cultural sphere, they all ended up, eventually, powerful enough to effect a radical change in both the legal structure of the constitution as well as in the cultural construction of the national identity formation.

Thus, in Jeffersonian and Wolinian terms, these rebellious social move-ments exercised their right to revolution by creating new cultural forms that, considered cumulatively from a historical perspective, transformed the meaning of American identity in profound ways. From this vantage point, then, we can recognize that of the underlying purposes of Jef-ferson's revolutionary rhetoric was to enable Americans to think more perceptively about initiating processes of constant political renewal in a peaceful manner.

As the introduction set forth, Jefferson understood that the purposes of public education had to be directed toward the civic formation of demo-cratic personalities—that is, toward the creation of new cultural identities

[6] See, for example, Johann Neem, *Democracy's Schools: The Rise of Public Education in America*. Baltimore: Johns Hopkins University Press, 2017.

as a precondition for the revolution to actualize itself over time. The chief reason why the establishment of public education assumed the status of a moral imperative for Jefferson, was his deep appreciation of the many ways in which the feudal and monarchical social imaginary still exerted ideological power over the national identity—even decades after the country's formal independence. The public schools were therefore envisioned to be transformational launch sites for initiating America's necessary revolution in mind and morals.

The historically novel civic formation of identity that Jefferson wanted to bring into existence through his educational proposals would be secular and republican in spirit. Such an education would be designed to create individuals intelligent enough to recognize ambition and tyranny whenever they saw it, and ethically courageous enough "to exert their power against" such manifestations when they occurred.[7] Jefferson's understanding of civic education reflects a clear theory/practice dimension. In this regard, it bears repeating that the "action component" of Jefferson's idealized version of civic education constitutes a significant piece of his larger revolutionary theory, since it's regarded as step one in igniting processes of democratic transition on the ground, so to speak.

The year 1823 marks the last time that Jefferson opines on the subject of permanent revolution, at least explicitly. Jefferson returns to the theme of emphasizing the necessary inter-generational efforts that would be required to keep processes of revolution alive and moving. A related element of Jefferson's revolutionary thought included a scathing indictment of the European model of identity that, in his mind, could only reproduce a society of submissive sheep incapable of rebellion or autonomous action.

The generation which commences a revolution can rarely complete it. Habituated from their infancy to passive submission of body and mind to their kings and priests, they are not qualified when called on, to think and provide for themselves, and their inexperience, their ignorance and their bigotry make them instruments often, in the hands of the Bonapartes and Iturbides to defeat their own rights and purposes.[8]

[7] "Bill No. 79 For a More General Diffusion of Knowledge." In Roy J. Honeywell, *The Educational Work of Thomas Jefferson*. Cambridge: Harvard University Press, 1931, 199.

[8] Thomas Jefferson to John Adams September 4, 1823.

The two eighteenth-century revolutions that Jefferson participated in and witnessed—the American and French—contributed to his image of what a successful democratic revolution should look like: Not to be understood as a terminal event, but as an ongoing process of cultural transformation, one whose telos was pointed toward the greater democratization of cultural life. As Jefferson states so eloquently, it's rare to find any revolutionary generations in history that have been fortunate enough to have both "commenced and completed" a revolution. As a theorist of revolution, therefore, Jefferson seems to recommend that one should radically enlarge one's historical time frame when contemplating what it would mean to transition to democracy. What would it mean, for example, to conceive of the struggle for social change in explicitly inter-generational terms? Would we act any differently equipped with this insight? Although Jefferson could never have used the following analogy himself, there's a sense in which his revolutionary theory embodies the notion that the historical process is more accurately viewed as a movie than a snapshot—an interminable process in which a kaleidoscope of parts fluidly collide, interact, and change form.

Jefferson, the eternal optimist, believes in the promise of better futures because he has trust in the capacity of human beings—as essentially moral and social beings—to have their reason and civic virtue developed. Unlike most of his contemporaries, Jefferson assumed that human beings were educable, which is another way of saying he believed in their capacity for transformation. Below he seems to recommend that the all-important moral "sentiment" for revolution ought to be the focus of an inter-generational educational project. This "sentiment" for being open to revolution or, more broadly put, openness to moral and cultural renovation, reflects a crucial linkage between Jefferson's educational and revolutionary theory. Among other notable implications, it signals that, for Jefferson, the best education is one in which the cultivation of moral sensitivity would serve as the curriculum's (and larger societies') overriding purpose. Moreover, in the following passage, we see that it's a kind of sentiment that contains an "intuitive" dimension that can be educated into fruition. So that,

A younger, and more instructed race comes on, the sentiment becomes more and more intuitive, and a 4th, a 5th, or some subsequent one of the ever renewed attempts will ultimately succeed.[9]

It is extraordinary that Jefferson would gaze into his crystal ball and envision revolutionary processes exceeding 5 generations and more, made possible by the right kind of "instruction." The passage reflects an image of democracy as an interminable project, one that would have to be enacted and reenacted over centuries. The passage also suggests the intimate functional relation in Jefferson's thought between the idea of permanent revolution and its necessary corollary, that of education's role in building up civic characters whose capacities for revision would be capable of touching every dimension of life.

Rebellion Is a Good Thing: Or, How to Conserve the Tradition of Dissent?

Jefferson's strong commitment to the therapeutic effects of revolutionary dissent is aptly reflected in his belief that even poorly conceived rebellions could play a positive role in the healthy development of democratic cultural life. One would assume, of course, that well-founded and eloquently justified revolutions, such as the American, would meet with Jefferson's approval. But that even those rebellions deemed misguided are considered praiseworthy, indicates the depth of Jefferson's belief that the "spirit of resistance" is precisely that which keeps governments responsive to the changing needs of the people.

Most historians acknowledge that Shays' Rebellion, which broke out in western Massachusetts in 1785–1786, frightened elites in every state of the union. The self-described "regulators" of the Shaysite movement came close to toppling the government of Massachusetts. In response, a movement developed among elites to adopt a new constitution in order to "revise" the Articles of Confederation. The subsequent US Constitution, ratified in 1792, included putting into place new mechanisms of federal power to suppress future rebellions (mechanisms that were immediately used to militarily suppress the 1794 Whiskey Rebellion). It is remarkable

[9] Ibid.

that Jefferson stood virtually alone among the nation's leadership in interpreting Shays' Rebellion as something that should be welcomed and not feared.[10]

The character of this welcoming spirit toward rebellion is well-captured in a letter Jefferson wrote to Abigail Adams. She had earlier written to Jefferson expressing grave alarm about the Shays' Rebellion. Jefferson, however, pushes back against the hostility she had expressed about the rebels. He remarks that,

> The spirit of resistance to government is so valuable on certain occasions, that I wish it always to be kept alive. It will often be wrong, but better so than not to be exercised at all. I like a little rebellion now and then. It is like a storm in the atmosphere.[11]

A few months later, in a letter to William Smith (1787), Jefferson returns to Shays' Rebellion:

> God forbid we should ever be 20 years without such a rebellion. The people cannot be all & always, well informed. The part which is wrong will be discontented in proportion to the importance of the facts they misconceive. If they remain quiet under such misconceptions it is a lethargy, the forerunner of death to the public liberty.[12]

To further grasp the underlying premises of Jefferson's cyclical theory of the "need" to have a revolution every 20 years, it's necessary to direct attention to his striking and related proposition that the "Earth belongs to the living."[13] Based on several letters Jefferson penned on the subject, this roughly twenty-year divide signaled for him a natural shift in generational ideas, power, and ownership. As an older generation died in sufficient numbers, the symbolic torch of historical ownership would be passed on to a younger generation. The use of such a generational marker, as an

---

[10] See Sean Condon, "Shays's Rebellion and the Constitution." In *Shays's Rebellion: Authority and Distress in Post-Revolutionary America*. Baltimore: Johns Hopkins University Press, 2015, 119–132.

[11] Thomas Jefferson (in Paris) to Abigail Adams, February 22, 1787.

[12] Thomas Jefferson (in Paris) to William Smith, November 13, 1787.

[13] For an indispensable discussion of Jefferson's proposed land reforms and their connection to his revolutionary theory, see Richard Matthews, *The Radical Politics of Thomas Jefferson*. Lawrence: University of Kansas Press, 1984, 19–29.

actuarial contrivance, represents a theoretical cornerstone of Jefferson's revolutionary theory. It is a bit complicated to explain how such a marker might be formally enacted in public policy terms. But understood as a rhetorical trope—"the earth belongs to the living"—seems to be deployed by Jefferson to theorize and help bring into being a kind of culture that would have a core element of *receptivity to change* built into its sociological DNA, as it were. Although Jefferson used the phrase in his campaign to uproot the feudal system of land tenure in Virginia, as we shall soon see, *the earth belongs to the living* also has intriguing implications at the level of ideological inheritance and critique.

To illustrate the strategic uses of the phrase, Jefferson and his political allies in Virginia, soon after the revolution concluded, moved swiftly to abolish the feudal legal practices of entail and primogeniture. The abolition of entail meant that land would now become available for use by the present generation, while the abolition of primogeniture meant, according to Staughton Lynd, that all of the present generations might use property equally.[14] Both of these feudal institutions seem somewhat complicated and foreign to our modern ears. Yet they were widely regarded by the revolutionary generation to represent *the* legal and economic foundation for the entrenchment of aristocratic privilege. The abolition of these legal privileges in Virginia and other states certainly did not end conditions of class inequality in the early republic. Yet, attempts were made in that direction. So even as Jefferson and his allies were successful in abolishing entail and primogeniture, the one piece of legislation removed from their larger bill was the distribution of 50 acres of land to every propertyless white adult male residing within Virginia. Although this egalitarian land reform was legislatively defeated, the point is that this widely overlooked proposal fits into Jefferson's larger theory of permanent revolution, as his image of revolutionary takeoff was premised on the amelioration of stark economic inequalities.[15]

This Jeffersonian piece of public rhetoric—the earth belongs to the living—expresses the idea that no generation at any level of analysis should be beholden to their "barbarous ancestors." Thus, while the phrase was

[14] See Staughton Lynd, *Intellectual Origins of the American Radicalism*. New York: Vintage Books, 1968, 77–85.

[15] Matthews, 27–29.

originally intended to spur much needed land reforms, Jefferson also intended it to encourage each generation to refresh the meaning of the nation's democratic ideals independently from their historically determined ideological inheritances, inheritances which, in Jefferson's view, were still deeply marked by monarchical and aristocratic influences. This meant that healthy republican cultures should never burden younger generations with their debt, their aristocratic privileges, their standing armies, or with any other ideologies deemed by the present generation to be obsolete. The earth belongs to the living is foundational to Jefferson's revolutionary vision because it was intended to encourage younger generations to declare independence from their forebears at every conceivable level—ideologically, morally, and educationally. Political theorist Judith Shklar nicely sums up the phrase's centrality to Jefferson's revolutionary theory:

> Every generation was new and unburdened with obligations to the past. Jefferson wanted not merely *new* politics, but a politics of perpetual *newness*, as implicit in democratic principles.[16]

Another cornerstone of Jefferson's revolutionary theory can be seen in his observation that the *absence* of rebellions, far from constituting a desirable social condition, is far more likely to symbolize the death of public liberty. Note how Jefferson surveys the country's political and cultural landscape in relation to the presence or absence of the spirit of resistance:

> We have had 13 states independent 11 years. There has been one rebellion. That comes down to one rebellion in a century & half for each state. What country before ever existed a century & half without a rebellion? & what country can preserve its liberties if their rulers are not warned from time to time that their people preserve the spirit of resistance? ...The tree of liberty must be refreshed from time to time by the blood of patriots and tyrants. It is its natural manure.[17]

Here Jefferson adopts nature and medicinal metaphors to convey the positive effects of rebellion on the body politic. In an oft-quoted letter to

---

[16] See, Judith N. Shklar, "Democracy and the Past: Jefferson and His Heirs." In *Redeeming American Political Thought*, ed. Stanley Hoffmann and Dennis F. Thompson. Chicago: University of Chicago Press, 1998, 174.

[17] Thomas Jefferson (in Paris) to William Smith, November 13, 1787.

James Madison (1787), he invokes the same imagery: "I hold it that a little rebellion now and then is a good thing, & as necessary in the political world as storms in the physical." Jefferson concludes the letter by writing that rebellion is a "medicine necessary for the sound health of government."[18] For Jefferson, rebellions in the social world are interpreted as natural, inevitable occurrences, not unlike weather itself. Even as Jefferson seems to locate rebellions as a phenomenon of the natural world, he recognizes that their manifestations in history are by no means automatic. Rather, the species of rebellion he appears to privilege would depend on the civic agency of individuals acting in purposeful solidarity—not toward any generic purpose—but only toward democratic–republican purposes.

While Jefferson preferred non-violent peaceful rebellions, he had no qualms about accepting the legitimacy of bloodshed as a part of the price paid for radical social transformation. Several letters he wrote during the French Revolution, to which he had a ringside seat, make clear that he was willing to accept the role of violence in social transformation. In writing to William Short (1793), Jefferson states that he was deeply impressed by the leaders of the French Revolution that they would, in their wisdom, "set fire to the four corners of the Kingdom and to perish with it themselves rather than to relinquish an iota from their plan of a total change in government."[19] Jefferson never wavered from his view that the blood-soaked French Revolution was a noble and necessary event. In the thick of the French Revolution, he declared that rather than watch the French Revolution fail, he would prefer to see "half the earth desolated. Were there but an Adam and Eve left in every country, and left free, it would be better than as it is now." From this, we can fairly surmise that Jefferson's revolutionary theory reserves a legitimate space for violence, provided, of course, that any given revolution's purposes is devoted to the creation and preservation of republican experiments.

Jefferson adds yet another interesting dimension to his revolutionary theory when he identifies the ever-present possibility of Americans acquiescing uncritically to self-congratulatory patriotic attitudes. For one of the country's most distinguished constitutional scholars to encourage the development of critical attitudes toward the meaning of the founding

---

[18] Thomas Jefferson (in Paris) to James Madison, January 30, 1787.

[19] Thomas Jefferson to William Short, January 3, 1793.

texts of the country, should qualify as impressive. Jefferson, in an oft-quoted phrase, criticizes those attitudes that would regard the US Constitution as the political equivalent of religious scripture:

> Some men look at constitutions with sanctimonious reverence, and deem them like the arc of the covenant, too sacred to be touched. They ascribe to the men of the preceding age a wisdom more than human, and suppose what they did to be beyond amendment.[20]

Jefferson offers a critique of the kind of cultural dispositions that could only stymie fresh, revisionary thinking. Below, Jefferson zeros in on what is perhaps the moral and conceptual foundation of his revolutionary thought:

> But I know also, that laws and institutions must go hand in hand with the progress of the human mind. As that becomes more developed, more enlightened, as new discoveries are made, new truths disclosed, and manners and opinions change with the change of circumstances, institutions must advance also, and keep pace with the times. We might as well require a man to wear still the coat which fitted him as a boy, as civilized society to remain ever under the regimen of their barbarous ancestors.[21]

The underlying focus of this passage directs our attention to the *human mind* and its *capacity for growth*. The coat metaphor illustrates how foundational the evolution of human consciousness is to Jefferson's political and educational thought. He seems to be arguing that without honoring this feature of human nature—the mind's capacity to revise itself over time—we couldn't really speak of the possibility of moral progress, or of transitions toward democracy. As many observers have rightly noted, Jefferson is a product of the enlightenment era, an era whose influences are central to Jefferson's notion of permanent revolution. His revolutionary theory, or rhetoric (by whatever name we choose to call it) is clearly yoked to a set of enlightenment assumptions about the foundational social

---

[20] Thomas Jefferson to Samuel Kerchival, July 12, 1816.
[21] Ibid.

and moral character of human beings. For Jefferson, and for other inter-preters of the enlightenment tradition, it is the social and moral character of humans that make something called "progress" possible.[22]

Another foundational assumption of Jefferson's theory that requires critical attention, is that the "permanent change" so often attributed to the Natural world, implies that processes of "permanent revolution" in social relations similarly constitute a reflection of Natural law. There is a sense in which the symmetry between permanent social change and the laws of Nature, provides Jefferson with a kind of scientific imprimatur to his revolutionary theory. As was mentioned in the Introduction, the aims and objectives of Jefferson's educational innovations are rooted in his idea about the reality or self-evident truth of permanent change. Accord-ing to Jefferson, while the laws of Nature never change, human societies and their corresponding forms of individual and collective consciousness, embedded as they are in historical time, always exist in states of ceaseless change. I would submit, then, that Jefferson wanted to morally renovate the colonial curriculum that he and others inherited, in such a way that it would be in close alignment with this scientific fact. The question of what it might mean today to align the curriculum in relation to this sci-entific fact, is a theme taken up in subsequent chapters, particularly in Chapter 11.

The viability of Jefferson's framework of permanent revolution, under-stood both as a social theory and as a rhetorical practice, relies in large part on his hope that an institutional structure of public education would someday come into existence to effectively distribute the "mass diffu-sion of knowledge" throughout American society. Simply put, there could be no other adequate institutional means for creating an intelligent and engaged public. Jefferson's commitment to public education as the best available means for the development of democratic selfhood and political culture constitutes the moral keystone of his overall educational vision.

---

[22] See, Stephen Eric Bronner, *Reclaiming the Enlightenment: Toward a Politics of Rad-ical Engagement.* New York: Columbia University Press, 2004. As Bronner contends, the enlightenment, as a contested signifier, is virtually impossible to frame as a monolithic tradition. That said, we can still generalize that one of its salutary characteristics is its crit-ical, dissent-friendly, revisionary strand which, as suggested, stems from our foundational essence as social and moral beings.

Another vital piece of this vision, however, has yet to be examined: The relationship between Jefferson's theory of permanent revolution, on the one hand, and "education" understood as those educational experiences occurring outside the boundaries of formal schooling, on the other. This feature of Jefferson's educational thought—namely, his wish for a broader American *paedeia* to take root and flourish—occupies a prominent place within his revolutionary theory.[23] Jefferson, in other words, wanted the social arrangements of society to be educative in their own right, beyond the boundaries of formal schooling.

IMAGES OF REVOLUTION AS DEMOCRATIC IMMANENCE

For Jefferson, the formation of such a *paideia* was vital to the continued existence of the republican experiment. Despite the fact that Jefferson does not make use of the Greek concept of *paideia* by name, we are on firm ground in positing that this term captures a core aim of Jefferson's philosophy of education. Jefferson affirms this vision with the articulation of a compelling truth claim: "If a nation expects to be ignorant and free," he observes, "it expects what never was and never will be."[24] Indeed, if power was in fact lodged with the People, the People had to *become* intelligent and alert, otherwise the exercise of their majority power would regress in the direction of an authoritarian tyranny. Jefferson's vision for reproducing intelligent and alert republicans in this broader cultural sense, can be seen when he refers to the educational import of newspapers, libraries, and other sources of free and publicly available information. In addition to extolling the virtues of newspapers, libraries, and the like, Jefferson also viewed the activity of civic participation as something potentially educative in and of itself.

The critical theorist Michael Hardt does a marvelous job of reminding us that Jefferson's educational theory should not be restricted to the

---

[23] To clarify: While Jefferson does not invoke the term, a concept of *paideia* is implicit in Jefferson's revolutionary thought when he, for example, attempts to foster the development of institutions (libraries, newspapers, schools) that will result in enlarging the public's intelligence. For the best traditional definition of this important concept, see Werner Jaeger, *Paideia: The Ideals of Greek Culture*, Vol. 2. New York: Oxford University Press, 1943, xii–xxix.

[24] Thomas Jefferson to Charles Yancey, January 6, 1816.

domain of formal education alone. Hardt argues that Jefferson recognized that experiences of participating in social and civic activities could be educative, and thus potentially transformative, in powerful ways. The content or substance of such non-formal, "street level" education is difficult to quantify, insofar as we cannot foresee the outcomes that activities of civic participation might produce. While the educational effects of civic engagement can only be partially foreseen and measured, Jefferson was nonetheless confident that they were vital to the progressive development of a revisionary, intelligent, and morally virtuous citizenry.

Hardt's interpretation of this strand of Jefferson's theory merits extended quotation:

> What is most important about Jefferson's conception of the revolutionary process, however, is not its temporal figure but its substance. The real core revolutionary event is the metamorphosis of the multitude, its developing new skills, knowledge's, and habits necessary to rule itself without masters, along with the expansion of its imagination and desire for democracy. The revolutionary event is not a contentless abyss and it does not come from the outside; it is an immanent process, a learning of democracy by doing it, a self-transformation.[25]

Hardt nicely captures the transformational thrust of Jefferson's democratic vision: that citizens should be "participators in public affairs not just on election day, but every day." Jefferson says this not only because he wants an intelligent and broadly engaged public to come into formation, but also because he appreciates that such participatory experiences can instigate new expressions of political creativity. These types of experiences, if multiplied a thousandfold, for example, would tend toward *raising* the consciousness of the multitude, thus serving to energize revolutionary processes of inter-generational growth. For Jefferson, such an education is moral through and through: the social/civic-oriented experiences one has tends to broaden one's outlook and alter one's symbolic identification with the broader public and thus with images of the common good. Jefferson recognizes that such expansions of knowledge and

[25] Michael Hardt, "Thomas Jefferson, Or, the Transition of Democracy." In *Thomas Jefferson: The Declaration of Independence*. London: Verso Books 2007, viii–xxv.

perspective should be encouraged beyond the confines of formal education.[26]

Hardt's analysis of Jefferson's revolutionary theory focuses primarily on the problem of transition, that is, the problem of what happens once any given revolutionary movement is able to constitute itself as a state power. Hardt interprets the modern historical record as it relates to the difficulties all revolutions face when transitioning toward democracy, or any other regime change. Hardt identifies the recurring tendency in modern revolutions to either devour themselves in anarchy (such as the French Revolution), or to create vast totalitarian bureaucracies (such as the Russian Revolution). The former ended in the Napoleonic dictatorship, while the latter no longer exists. Although these modern revolutions produced their own theorists focused on the problem of managing their respective post-revolution transitions, notably Robespierre, Lenin, and Trotsky, according to Hardt's analysis, the French and Russian Revolutions crashed on the jagged shoals of their post-revolution transitions.[27]

In Hardt's view, the American revolution, while less radical in some ways than the French or Russian, fares better when viewed from a longer historical perspective (the criterion that ought to count most). The American revolution "survived" as a process in part because novel mechanisms of transition and revision were built into the nation's founding legal documents, notably the amendment process and the ongoing debates instigated by the moral ideals put into circulation by the preamble of the Declaration and the Constitution. The sublime democratic rhetoric contained in these texts, despite the fact that the phrases and principles have never really been legally binding in a constitutional sense, still have exercised a morally energizing impact on both the formation of American political culture and negotiations over the meaning of national identity.

What Hardt admires most about Jefferson is that he sought a theoretical way out of the dilemmas of revolutionary transition. With Jefferson's conceptual innovation, there is no beginning, middle, or end to the revolutionary process. The original revolutionary event ceases to be a onetime affair, precisely the historiographical insight emphasized in the Introduction. As Hardt writes, "each generation must keep the spirit of revolution

---

[26] If this paragraph sounds a lot like John Dewey, it is because Dewey's educational thought is rooted in Jefferson's own experimentalism, a theme discussed in Chapter 4.

[27] Hardt, ix–xii.

alive by rebelling against the government, revising the constitution, and reopening the constituent process."[28] The only way to keep the revolution going, in other words, is to repeat it. Yet, the repetition should not be construed as identical to the original event. The defining moral ideals remain the same—equality, democracy, dissent, and so on—but their meanings have to be remade and reapplied in historical contexts in which new human needs have arisen (a point which Dewey beautifully captures in the final pages of Chapter 4).

An additional innovation that Hardt identifies in Jefferson's revolutionary theory is his idea that the *ends* of democracy cannot be separated from the *means* employed to attain them. As noted above, it is on this "jagged shoal" that most revolutions have ultimately failed. For example, as Hardt observes, the Russian Revolution's leadership invented the "dictatorship of the proletariat" to serve as a temporary means of rule until the consciousness of the people was sufficiently raised so that, they too, could, at some indefinite future point, rule themselves without masters. However, as was the case with the USSR, the hoped for "withering away of the state" never materialized. The means employed to further the Russian Revolution were severely divorced from its stated ends, thus dooming it as a revolutionary project.

As distinct from any revolutionary approach in which the ends and means are unimportant or confused beyond recognition, then, the important thing to remember for now is that education, understood in both its formal and informal expressions, reveals itself as the primary (though not the only) *means* through which the *ends* of democracy might be achieved. In this sense, the "real revolutionary event" for Jefferson is exemplified through the agency of education, as when there is a "constant self-making of the multitude." This theme of bringing together the means of education for the ends of democracy will be further examined in Chapters 4 and 5 from a Jefferson-inspired, Deweyan and Countsian perspective.

[28] Ibid., ix–xii.

SCIENCE, ENLIGHTENMENT,
AND PERMANENT REVOLUTION

As is well known, Jefferson not only loved scientific inquiry, he loved the possibility that public happiness in America could be expanded were scientific endeavor to be guided by republican rather than elite purposes. He said on several occasions that the contemplation and practice of science, its inquiries, experiments, discoveries, and inventions constituted one of his "supreme delights."[29] That scientific inquiry and its findings would rise to the level of a supreme delight for a sitting president is admirable, especially from a contemporary perspective. In any case, the expansion of science into multiplying fields of knowledge during the Age of Enlightenment gave Jefferson the confidence that the future would surely be brighter than the past. If the scientific method of experimentation could be more energetically applied to address the problems of (sic) man, Jefferson wrote, and if its spirit of discovering new truths could be more energetically embodied within the nascent American culture, he was confident the nation's experiment in democracy would succeed. Indeed, his frequent reference to the nation's "experiment" with self-government tacitly invokes the scientific method, thus offering another example of how Jefferson's political discourse was shaped in large part by his passion for the fruits of scientific inquiry. Moreover, the historian of science, I. Bernard Cohen, asserts that the language of the Declaration of Independence, particularly its appeal to "the laws of nature," echo a familiarity with the Newtonian literature of his day.[30]

Jefferson's idea of permanent revolution is directly linked to his commitment to science as a defining human activity: that is, the activity of pursuing the truth of how the laws of nature operate. He believed that, properly construed, the scientific method could itself serve as a vehicle of permanent revolution. As new forms of knowledge and truth were discovered, as we saw in his letter to Kercheval, such knowledge acquisition would create the conditions in which existing forms of culture, politics, and law would require reformulation to keep pace with the steady advances of scientific knowledge (including technological innovation).

---

[29] Thomas Jefferson to DuPont de Nemours, March 3, 1809.

[30] I. Bernard Cohen, *Science and the Founding Fathers: Science in the Political Thought of Jefferson, Franklin, Adams and Madison.* New York: W. W. Norton & Norton Company, 1999, 114.

Jefferson declared that "science is more important in a republican than any other form of government,"[31] because he saw science as a pursuit whose cumulative effects could help foster a citizenry committed to notions of "objective truth" as well as to a political culture receptive to continual renewal as those truths changed. Regarding the politics of science, Jefferson believed that, to the extent the benefits of science accrued only to the elite classes, as they did in Europe, the value of scientific research conducted for the benefit of the broader public, would be squandered. On this rather profound point, John Dewey recognized that Jefferson's interpretation of the proper purposes of science were, at bottom, democratic. Dewey writes that, "Just as the 'people' in whom he trusted as the foundation and ultimate security of self-governing institutions, so it was the enlightenment of the people as a whole which was his aim in promoting the advance of science."[32]

The reproductive linkages between the American Revolution, science, and the future of the nation's democratic experiment are highlighted in a letter Jefferson wrote a few weeks before his death. He begins by stating that the American Revolution signaled to the entire world that human beings were not intended to be bound by chains to "monkish ignorance and superstition," for it had "restored the free right to the unbounded exercise of reason and freedom of opinion." Jefferson observes that, "the general spread of the light of science has already laid open to every view the palpable truth that the mass of mankind has not been born with saddles on their backs, nor a favored few booted and spurred, ready to ride them legitimately, by the grace of God."[33] It's remarkable that Jefferson would so explicitly connect the "light of science" and its ability to produce "palpable truths" to the *ideological* unmasking of the ancient regime.

As Jefferson peered into the unknowable future, he expressed hope that the possibilities of scientific inquiry (and the arts) would do much to promote the overall happiness of American society. In an 1818 letter, for example, he identifies science as a developing institution central to the project of transcending the established order:

---

[31] Thomas Jefferson to [unknown correspondent], September 28, 1821. Quoted from Jennings L. Wagoner, *Jefferson and Education*. Chapel Hill: University of North Carolina Press, 2004, 53.

[32] John Dewey, *Presenting Thomas Jefferson*. New York: Longmans, Green and Co. 1940, 11.

[33] Thomas Jefferson to Roger C. Weightman, June 24, 1826.

When I contemplate the immense advances in science and discoveries in the arts which have been made within the period of my life, I look forward with confidence to equal advances by the present generation, and have no doubt they will consequently be much wiser than we have been as we than our fathers were and they than the burners of witches.[34]

Jefferson's generational retrospective here is emblematic of his revolutionary theory, whereby an American culture goes from burning witches to embracing science. It nicely illustrates why Jefferson thought that scientific inquiry, and its findings, had an indispensable role to play in the progressive evolution of American democracy.

SUMMARY

Based on our review of Jefferson's revolutionary theory, let us hazard a few generalizations about the concept. Although Jefferson's rhetorical approach for expressing his views are unsystematically presented, they nonetheless reflect a set of moral visions and democratic aims that go some distance in conveying what Jefferson was trying to "get at" in developing the idea of permanent revolution. We have seen how the concept contains profound if unexplored political and educational implications. We see in Jefferson's writings, for example, the idea that democratic revolutions depend for their existence on increasing the intelligence of the people, whose intelligence, in turn, depends on the people's deepening civic participation, or as Danielle Allen calls it, on their "participatory readiness."[35] This civic participation of citizens is framed by Jefferson as the precondition for ongoing political renewal. While the notion of free public education was seen as vital in encouraging civic participation as a moral ideal, it's also the case that Jefferson understands that such participation occurring outside the confines of formal school settings could be educative in its own right. The emergence of greater levels of civic agency, whether emanating from inside or outside the schools, was regarded as the basis for catalyzing creative transitions toward democracy. Jefferson's revolutionary theory, then, is conceptually holistic. To begin to map its

[34] Thomas Jefferson to Dr. Waterhouse, March 3, 1818.

[35] Danielle Allen, What Is Education For? *Boston Review*, May 2106. Allen's concept of "participatory readiness" will be invoked in several chapters owing to my judgement that it perfectly captures Jefferson's moral ideal for citizenship.

conceptual boundaries, we could describe Jefferson's theory by locating it at the intersection where the moral, political, educational, and scientific converge: These categories are woven into a modernist cloth through Jefferson's deft rhetorical skills.

As Hardt emphasizes, Jefferson is radical as a theorist in his belief that America's revolution should be seen foremost as a study in democratic immanence: that is, as that which occurs when individuals and cultures undertake unceasing efforts to raise the consciousness and promote the general welfare of the People. Broadly put, this unceasing effort, this ongoing expression of *demophilia*, represents the moral cornerstone of Jefferson's concept of permanent revolution (even if he didn't use this exact term).[36] Without this transformational moral element of educational purpose being privileged within the nation's political culture, the magnificent yet elusive Spirit of 76 would inevitably be prone to degeneration—or so Jefferson thought. Assuming that this mythopoetic field of meaning has degenerated to the point of near symbolic death today, in Parts II and III we will examine alternative approaches for promoting that spirit's regeneration. Equipped with this broad conception of Jefferson's revolutionary theory, we turn now to explore the ways in which Jefferson's educational proposals can be seen to fit into the larger mosaic of his revolutionary theory.

[36] The term—*demophilia*, or "love of the people"—is taken from George Counts as expressed in his *A Call to the Teachers of the Nation* (see Chapter 5 for more on this theme). I am also indebted to Unger and West for their definition of the term and how they frame it in the context of US history. See, Roberto Unger and Cornel West, *The Future of American Progressivism*. Boston: Beacon Press, 1998, 12.

readiness."[1] Allen's concept of participatory readiness is deeply Jeffersonian. Its essential meaning aligns perfectly with what Jefferson wanted to achieve through his educational proposals. In the pages ahead, I discuss how these two related moral ideals, revisability, and participatory readiness, represent two sides of the same ontological coin and signify vital experiential outcomes of Jefferson's educational project.

We could tentatively define revisability as a capacity that, while intrinsic to all human beings, also signifies a developmental or educable potential. However intrinsic this human potential may be, there's no guarantee that it will manifest itself automatically. The idea of revisability as a moral ideal can be interpreted as an individual's capacity for psychological growth and transformation, a psychic experience that, among other things, requires conscious "exercise" toward processes of learning, unlearning, and relearning. This all-important human propensity toward *individual* transformation may be usefully understood as the metaphoric square root for catalyzing larger *social* transformations in the cultural and political sphere.

To further illustrate this point, let's consider what the national identity would look like today had Americans been unwilling to exercise their capacity to revise themselves over time. In this dystopian hypothetical, we would still have slavery, women would not be citizens, only white male property owners would qualify for citizenship, and public education wouldn't exist. This brief snapshot reminds us not only of the oligarchic, racist, and patriarchal origins of the national identity formation, but also the degree to which the American people have been willing and able to engage in acts of political creativity. It should be noted that the dissenting social movements which gave rise to these historical transformations, all aimed toward the expansion of citizenship and equal participation— and all representing fluid transitions toward democracy—precisely those qualities that Jefferson attempts to capture in his revolutionary theory.

So, the ultimate aim of "transforming the consciousness of the multitude" (to borrow from Hardt's formulation) can be seen as one of, if not *the* organizing principle of Jefferson's educational and political thought. This organizing principle, with its focus on revolution as an ongoing moral event, signifies why Jefferson's theory can be regarded as one of the most revolutionary legacies of the American Revolution. Within this

---

[1] Danielle Allen, "What Is Education For?" *Boston Review*, May 9, 2016, pp. 8, 3, 9.

historiographic tradition, on my reading, the success of the American Revolution is not to be judged by its successful seizure of state power, but rather by the ability of that founding event to inspire new and revisionary incarnations of its underlying moral character. On both historical and theoretical grounds, then, I think we can safely infer that the capacity to revise (including the willingness, or desire, to revise) can be interpreted as foundational to democratic culture and education. Simply put: Acting on our capacities to revise is what enables formally democratic persons and cultures to actually *be* democratic.

Jefferson's ideas about the value of education and ideological dissent in a democratic republic did not emerge from thin air. He learned invaluable lessons from his study of the ancient Greek experience with democracy.[2] The political theorist Josiah Ober, in his incisive interpretations of democratic political culture in ancient Athens, writes that the capacity and willingness to revise and experiment was perhaps the defining feature of the Athenian, always-in-the-making, democratic regime.[3] The presence of these improvisational and experimental qualities stemmed in large part from the assumption that the laws that governed Athens contained absolutely no metaphysical or religious foundation. Instead, it was broadly understood that fallible human beings made fallible laws, and because this was the case, the Athenians had no qualms about frequently revising the laws. In rejecting a religious or metaphysical conception of law as the dominant vehicle for organizing their polis, the ancient Athenians provided Jefferson with a valuable historical model for effectuating a similar transition 2000 years later on American soil.[4]

Ober is emphatic that "major revisions" undertaken in democratic regimes, require political cultures that have learned to accept and value

---

[2] It is well known that Jefferson read Greek and Latin in the original and, like other founders, was deeply acquainted with thinking about the virtues and vices of democratic, republican, and mixed political models. See, for example, Carl J. Richard, *Greeks and Romans Bearing Gifts: How the Ancients Inspired the Founding Fathers*. Rowman & Littlefield, 2008.

[3] Josiah Ober, "How to Criticize Democracy in Late Fifth-and Fourth-Century Athens." In *The Athenian Revolution: Essays on Ancient Greek Democracy and Political Theory*. Princeton University Press, 1998, 140–160.

[4] For a cogent discussion of this defining feature of democratic Athens, see Cornelius Castoriadis, "The Problem of Democracy Today." *Democracy & Nature*, Vol. 8, 1995, 18–37.

criticism from individuals and groups operating outside of the dominant political culture:

> The regime that is to maintain its flexibility must allow social space exterior to itself: if a political system could ever encompass the whole of society and the whole field of discourse, it would lose its capacity for self-generated change.[5]

Ober's interpretation makes clear that a genuinely democratic culture must validate and honor its dissenters. Here, we can interpret the death penalty meted out to Socrates for corrupting the youth to be an instructive failure on the part of Athenian democracy to properly value dissent as a moral ideal. Thus, for democratic cultures, valuing dissent and dissenters is something of a complex achievement. We need to learn to value the perspective of the so-called outsiders because they are usually the first ones to see the problems and needs that everyone else is content to ignore. Seeming to have appreciated the perennial democratic imperative to value dissent, Jefferson wrote on many occasions that the American experiment in self-government would inevitably decay were it ever to lose its capacity for self-critique.

Although the capacity and willingness to revise at the individual level is paramount to the formation of viable democratic republics, this feature cannot be so easily teased apart from other, equally important human capacities and qualities. As was suggested in the Introduction, the personal qualities of being experimental, critical, and of having a historical awareness, are corollary civic virtues that a Jeffersonian-inspired education is designed to bring into being. The constellation of educable capacities and qualities that I have identified and generalized from Jefferson's theory—for them to achieve conceptual coherence—need to be recognized as working in a relationship, synergistically. Put in the form of a proposition: the human *capacity* to revise, when coupled with the moral or ethical *willingness* to revise, can result in creating a sense of participatory readiness. This marvelous democratic state of mind can emerge more readily when individuals have their experimental, critical, and historical faculties robustly exercised.

With these preliminary reflections in mind, the following sections of the chapter examine select dimensions of Jefferson's educational writings

[5] Ober, 142.

and discuss how they do their work in terms of rounding out the educational pieces of his revolutionary theory. I throw light on the Jeffersonian construction of educational purpose in a general sense, and then articulate how its overriding civic purposes function as the keystone of his revolutionary theory. The final section discusses Jefferson's so-called moral sense philosophy, an interpretive approach that underpins his evolutionary theories regarding the intricate dynamics of human social relations. This loosely knit enlightenment philosophy, at one level, embodies Jefferson's optimistic assumptions about the possibilities of human potential; at another, it provides a moral foundation for justifying his civic and humanities-friendly construction of educational purpose.

REMEMBERING THE CIVIC SPIRIT OF JEFFERSON'S EDUCATIONAL *DEMOPHILIA*

With the release of the Declaration of Independence on July 4, 1776, Jefferson and his revolutionary cohorts certainly ventured into uncertainty. While armed conflict had already commenced at Lexington and Concord in April 1775, the public readings of the Declaration in all 13 states made a wider war inevitable. Among the many other urgent tasks that required immediate attention (in addition to organizing a national military) was that of revising each of the now obsolete 13 state constitutions. Thus, after finishing his rhetorical handiwork in Philadelphia, Jefferson was anxious to return to Virginia to "lay the axe," as he put it, to its feudal and monarchical constitution. Jefferson wanted to pave the way for future revolutionary transition by establishing in its place a secular legal structure grounded in republican values and principles.

Overall, Jefferson and his colleagues succeeded in abolishing some of the defining features of Virginia's state constitution. One of their most radical legal revisions was to dis-establish, from the state, the church's myriad legal, economic, and social privileges, an innovation which presaged the constitutional separation of church and state embodied in the First Amendment to the US Constitution (1791).

An immediate problem that Jefferson faced, however, was that the few schools which did exist in the colonial period operated under private religious control. Jefferson was convinced that, if the church-based schools in Virginia and the sister states were to continue to play the dominant role in educating the young, they would continue to reproduce religious hierarchies and rigid class-based divisions. In Jefferson's mind, there could be no ongoing revolution without first ending the virtual monopolies that religious institutions enjoyed in the realm of education and politics.

In wielding his legislative axe specifically against the old regime of education, Jefferson explicitly states in Bill No. 79 that the education of the young should be conducted within publically funded spaces, spaces that were envisioned to provide a certain kind of moral equality between rich and poor children.[6] On the basis of Jefferson's educational renovations, we could say that, going forward, the nation's *construction of educational purpose* was going to be made on behalf of the public's interest, rather than on behalf of thousands of different private church-based interests. This public/private distinction in relation to education is crucial. For under Jefferson's plan, the young would be educated, above all, as potentially virtuous citizens, and not as congregants in this or that religious denomination. Jefferson understood that the success of his broader project of permanent transition toward democracy would depend on each of the states' adopting similar constitutional revisions as a means to liberate future generations from anti-republican and anti-scientific forms of education.

As noted, the defining general features of Jefferson's educational theory can be readily gleaned from his Bill No. 79 for The More General Diffusion of Knowledge (1779). The title of the bill itself is worth pausing over. It represents a symbolic declaration of independence from all previous aristocratic educational regimes whose very existence—at least according to Jefferson—necessarily rested on the enforcement of mass ignorance. In an eighteenth-century context, therefore, it was exceptional for Jefferson to propose a set of laws that not only mandated a system of publicly funded education, but also mandated its civic purposes for the goal of creating an intelligent public. While we could accurately point out that Jefferson's modest K-3 educational design reflects a pyramidal, overly meritocratic structure, the more vital point for this inquiry, is that the schools' underlying civic purpose was not intended to cement into place an artificial aristocracy based on birth, rank, and inherited privilege (as had been the case for centuries). Its purpose, rather, was to lay the institutional groundwork for leveling the playing field for rich and poor alike insofar as public schooling was concerned.

[6]Thomas Jefferson, Bill #79 for a More General Diffusion of Knowledge. In James B. Conant, *Thomas Jefferson and the Development of American Public Education*. Los Angeles: University of California Press, 1963, 88–93.

Bill No. 79 contains 19 sections and describes in detail how Jefferson's proposed educational system was to be locally administered according to scrupulous democratic procedures. In the bill, the amount of space devoted to the underlying philosophical and curricular purposes is relatively small compared to the lengthy and dense administrative statutes. For our purposes, it will be sufficient to examine the initial provisions that express the symbiotic relationship between education for human flourishing and the inter-generational project of permanent revolution.

Jefferson begins No. 79 by highlighting one of his foundational axioms whose conceptual roots are traced to the origins of the western tradition of political theory. Namely, that there is a law-like tendency among all governments, at all times, to gradually degenerate into tyranny: "...experience hath shown, that even under the best forms, those entrusted with power have, in time, and by slow operations, perverted it into tyranny."[7]

How, then, should governments confront the apparent inevitability of their own moral and political degradation? In the second clause of section I, Jefferson provides what he sees as the best remedy: "... and it is believed that the most effectual means for preventing this would be to illuminate the minds of the people at large."[8] Jefferson expresses the same ardent faith in the powers of education a few years later in a letter to George Wythe (1786), where he again frames the cultivation of intelligence and virtue among the people as the best safeguard against tyranny and the restoration of aristocratic rule:

> Preach, my dear sir, a crusade against ignorance; establish and improve the law for educating the common people. Let our countryman know, that the people alone can protect against these evils, and that the tax which will be paid for this purpose, is not more than the thousandth part of what will be paid to kings, priests and nobles, who will rise up among us if we leave the people in ignorance.[9]

For Jefferson, then, the gravest danger facing the nation—the loss of its republican identity—could be most effectively countered by creating institutions of education such as schools, libraries, and newspapers whose

---

[7] Ibid.

[8] Ibid.

[9] Jefferson (from Paris) to George Wythe, August 13, 1786.

chief purpose would be devoted to educating intelligent and participatory citizens (and leaders). It bears repeating here that for Jefferson and others in the revolutionary generation, the existence of aristocracies and monarchies relied in large part on their ability to maintain and enforce the ignorance of their subjects. At the most fundamental level, Jefferson's educational proposals sought to lift that historically rooted repression by diffusing knowledge broadly among the people, and this is how educating an intelligent public emerges as a central piece of broader revolutionary theory.

The following clause of section I of Bill No. 79 directs attention to the indispensable role that civic education must play if the United States was to survive as a republic. Jefferson suggests that knowledge of the past can foster within individuals a kind of ethical fortitude or moral receptivity that would encourage them to "take the right kind of actions." He argues that passage of the bill would

> ...especially give (citizens) knowledge of those facts, which history exhibiteth, that, possessed thereby of the experience of other ages and countries, they may be enabled to know ambition under all its shapes, and prompt to exert their natural powers to defeat its purposes.[10]

The reason why Jefferson emphasizes the histories of classical antiquity (as he does again in section VI) is not merely to fill students with rote or neutral knowledge about the "facts" of these subjects. Rather, historical study is regarded as an indispensable moral and political exercise: To the degree students are "enabled to know ambition under all its shapes," Jefferson argues, they would be more likely to "exert their natural powers to defeat its purposes."[11] In other words, Jefferson recommended this kind of education for the young not because he wanted them to be filled with mere facts about the past. In a deeper moral sense, he wanted to equip them with this knowledge *so that* they would be able and willing to act on behalf of what we could call the democratic values.

Unlike neoliberal forms of education today, whose seeming purpose is to provide students with amoral, apolitical forms of "neutral" knowledge, Jefferson argues for the development of a political knowledge consistent with the aims of reproducing citizens for intelligent life in a democratic

[10] Bill No. 79.
[11] Ibid.

republic. This Jeffersonian interpretation of political knowledge is given a cogent twentieth-century update by George S. Counts in the midst of the Great Depression, as we shall see in Chapter 5.

Jefferson theorizes an educational purpose that cannot be regarded as politically neutral. It appears, rather, the educational purpose that Jefferson envisions is guided by an end-in-view (telos) that's designed to produce a certain kind of political perspective *and* ethical action. Once we recognize that Jefferson's educational aims are anything but politically neutral, several questions arise. Would the implementation of Jefferson's educational blueprint, for example, embody a form of indoctrination? Is it "indoctrination," exactly, for the schools to stimulate abilities and form values in youth so that they may learn to judge, to choose, and to act on behalf of the democratic values?

In true enlightenment fashion, Jefferson wants to recruit and direct the positive power of the state to empower the intelligence and flourishing of the people as a whole. And while Jefferson is accurately identified to be an advocate of limited government, in this instance, he considered the active use of state power (including the federal government) to represent a legitimate force for bringing into being an intelligent public. As was observed in Chapter 2, Jefferson wants the people to be transformed through education to become not only more alert to the defense of their own interests and rights, but also to become co-participators in the ongoing experiment in democratic self-government. This sentiment is on display, for example, in the following letter, where Jefferson links the availability of free public education to his larger project of mobilizing a public to contribute to the perpetual renewal of the American Revolution:

> The object is to bring into action that mass of talents which lies buried in poverty in every country, for want of the means of development, and thus give activity to the mass of mind, which, in proportion to our population, shall be the double or treble of what it is in most countries.[12]

Jefferson's commitment to a civic and eudaimonist vision for American education, coupled with his faith in what the American people *might eventually become* as a result of such a commitment, can be seen to reflect

---

[12] Thomas Jefferson to J. Correa de Serra, November 25, 1817.

an underlying educational *demophilia*.[13] Jefferson never used the term *demophilia* to describe his underlying educational purposes. However, I think there are sufficient grounds to invoke the concept to capture the moral spirit underlying Jefferson's construction of educational purpose. Jefferson's educational proposals reflect a desire to foster the intelligence and happiness of the people; in addition, they reflect a belief in the capacity of the people *for* enlightenment. Obviously, we must first recognize that Jefferson's educational purposes only extended to white people and therefore were profoundly marred by racial exclusion. For the purposes of our inquiry, the chief problem here is with the narrow scope of application that Jefferson gave to his educational purposes. From a contemporary perspective, the moral spirit housed within the concept of *demophilia*, as defined above, clearly needs to be opened up and remade to work on behalf of all Americans today. Going forward, then, a non-racialized concept of *demophilia* should be articulated as one of the moral cornerstones of a newly constructed democratic paradigm of education.

HOW THE BUREAUCRATIC STRUCTURE OF JEFFERSON'S EDUCATIONAL PROPOSALS WERE RADICALLY DEMOCRATIC

After having briefly articulated the underlying civic purposes of the schools in Bill No. 79, Jefferson proceeds to detail, quite scrupulously, the bureaucratic structure of his educational legislation. He proposes that Virginia should institute a comprehensive system of publicly funded schools, where ultimate authority and control of them would rest with localized governments. Jefferson sought to divide the state into 42 counties; each county was to be sub-divided into political units which he refers to as wards. Based on population and geographic factors, there would be K-3 elementary schools distributed within these wards which Jefferson called hundreds. Significantly, in Section XI, Jefferson stipulates that every school building shall be constructed of "brick or stone," as if to morally concretize and render permanent the institution of free public education.

Jefferson was attempting to design a highly decentralized bureaucratic structure that would organize the schools administratively based

---

[13] In Greek, "eudaimonism" translates to happiness, one of the ultimate aims of Jefferson's educational philosophy according to Jefferson scholar M. Andrew Holowchak. See, his *Thomas Jefferson's Philosophy of Education: A Utopian Dream*. New York: Routledge, 2014, 145.

on democratic standards of equality and accountability. What makes Jefferson's educational proposals historically radical, in addition to the egalitarian moral purpose of promoting public intelligence, was the attempt to construct institutional bridges between the locally controlled school systems (hundreds) and the locally controlled political systems (wards). The holistic democratic architecture of such an arrangement is remarkable: its purpose was to educate both the young in the public schools *and* the adult citizens in the "schools" of self-government. Jefferson's historically innovative, yet ultimately defeated educational legislation, represents yet another foundational piece of his revolutionary vision. They are "foundational" insofar as the ongoing nature of the revolution was understood by Jefferson to depend on whether the state was prepared to actively foster the intelligence and participatory readiness of the people at a grass-roots level.

As Hannah Arendt articulated it, perhaps the most serious flaw that Jefferson spied in the Constitution was that it codified a timid mechanical version of citizenship limited to episodic acts of electing representatives.[14] Jefferson thus proposed the ward/hundred system to lay a foundation for countering what he regarded as the anti-democratic effects of the Constitution. Jefferson hoped that the ward system would introduce every citizen to participation in local government at one level or another.[15] The state-sponsored promotion of substantive or daily civic participation, beyond the merely procedural model of citizenship ordained within the Constitution, represents a key feature of Jefferson's educational vision. Arendt's interpretation of Jefferson permits us to see how the ward system and the schools located within the hundreds, when operating in unison, were intended to serve as institutional building blocks for amplifying civic participation and the public happiness of American society.

In a letter to John Adams, for example, Jefferson discusses how his educational vision constituted one piece of his larger democratic vision.

At the first session of our legislature after the Declaration of Independence, we passed a law abolishing entails. And this was followed by abolishing the privilege of primogeniture...These laws, drawn by myself, laid the axe to the root of pseudo-aristocracy. And had another, which I proposed, been adopted by the legislature, our work would have been complete.

[14] See Hannah Arendt, *On Revolution*. New York: Penguin, 1963, 233.
[15] Ibid., pp. 233, 253.

It was a bill for the more general diffusion of learning. This proposed to divide every county into wards of five or six miles square, like your townships, to establish in each ward a free school for reading, writing and common arithmetic, to provide for the annual selection of the best subjects from these schools, who might receive at the public expense a higher degree of education at a district school, and from these district schools to select a certain number of the most promising subjects, to be completed at a university where all the useful sciences should be taught. Worth and genius would thus have been sought out from every condition of life, and completely prepared by education for defeating the competition of wealth and birth for public trusts.[16]

While the educational reforms that Jefferson hints at here can be criticized as overly meritocratic, the larger point, in my estimation, is that Jefferson's statement reflects a holistic vision of a democratic America. Expanding on this vision a few years later to educational ally Joseph C. Cabell, Jefferson discusses why the structure of Virginia society, under his revisals, would have strengthened its republican character against the ever-present forces of wealth and corruption.

The elementary republics of the wards, the county republics, the State republics, and the republic of the Union, would form a gradation of authorities, standing each on the basis of law, holding every one of its delegated share of powers, and constituting truly a system of fundamental balances and checks for the government. *Where every man is a fundamental sharer in the direction of his ward republic, or of some of the higher ones, and feels that he is a participator in the government of affairs not merely at election, one day in the year, but every day;* when there shall not be a man in the state who will not be a member of some one of its councils, great or small, he will let the heart be torn out of his body, sooner than his power be wrested from him by a Caesar or Bonaparte.[17] (my italics)

Once again, Jefferson drives home the moral principle that democratic republics can only survive on the foundation of an intelligent, engaged citizenry. As previously discussed, Danielle Allen's normative goal of *participatory readiness* closely mirrors what Jefferson had envisioned as the

[16] Thomas Jefferson to John Adams, October 12, 1813.

[17] Thomas Jefferson to Joseph Cabell, February 2, 1816. The *italicized* passage is cited by Arendt twice as the foundation of Jefferson's revolutionary thought. See 127, 132, in *On Revolution.*

highest form of citizenship. For Jefferson, decentralizing the administration of the schools in concert with decentralizing the state into political sub-divisions was all about increasing civic participation so as to keep the revolution moving forward. Jefferson scholar Richard Matthews makes this point explicit when he observes that the new political spaces that were envisioned by Jefferson's revisals "is intimately linked with the maintenance of a spirit of revolution in the society at large."[18] According to Matthews, encouraging new forms of civic engagement would have the salutary effect of working against the formation of extreme inequalities of wealth.[19]

Moreover, the formation of both a stable middle class and a hospitable political and social environment would also carry profound implications for shaping images of the Self/Other relation. The historian Drew McCoy contends that a fair distribution of property was seen not only by Jefferson, but by the revolutionary generation in general, as necessary to the development among the people of a sense of the Common Good:

> ...the revolutionaries did not intend to provide men with property so that they might flee from public responsibility into a selfish privatism; property was rather the necessary basis for a committed republican citizenry.[20]

Given the deepening inequalities that bedevil American society today, it's well worth recalling that, among the best legacies of the American Revolution was the Jeffersonian idea that it was morally and legally legitimate for government to play a role in ensuring that wealth and property were more equitably distributed. Not only would such policies form a metaphorical "rudder" to stabilize the ship of state, but perhaps most significantly, it was only in the context of an egalitarian political and economic structure that citizens could realistically develop more benevolent, caring attitudes toward others.

[18] See Richard Matthews, *The Radical Politics of Thomas Jefferson*. Lawrence: University of Kansas Press, 1984, 85.

[19] Ibid., 24–29.

[20] Drew R. McCoy, *The Elusive Republic: Political Economy in Jeffersonian America*. Chapel Hill: University of North Carolina Press, 1996, 68.

RETRIEVING JEFFERSON'S MORAL SENSE PHILOSOPHY TO SERVE AS A FOUNDATION FOR RECONSTRUCTING THE PURPOSES OF PUBLIC EDUCATION IN THE UNITED STATES

The first aim of this section will be to provide a brief overview of Jefferson's moral and social interpretation of human nature, and to explain how it dovetails with the revisionary quality of his revolutionary theory. The second aim will be to suggest how Jefferson's moral sense philosophy could serve today as a moral foundation upon which to rearticulate the civic and moral purposes of American public education.

As was suggested in the Introduction, it may feel a bit strange to attribute a so-called "moral sense" philosophy to a figure like Jefferson. Despite Jefferson's rather tortured relationship to slavery, at least he seemed to acknowledge the humanity of the slaves themselves.[21] And, unlike most of his slave-holding brethren, Jefferson wrote poignantly about the ways in which slavery degraded slaves and slave-holders alike.[22] Jefferson's insightful critiques of the master/slave relation, coupled with his early efforts to legislate against the continuation of slavery in Virginia, may not impress readers today given the contradictions if not hypocrisies he could be said to personify. Nonetheless, Jefferson's recognition that slavery created an oppressive dialectical relation between master and slave reflects his moral sense philosophical approach, insofar as he recognized that the Self/Other relation is indivisibly connected.[23] As we shall see in the coming pages, the recognition that human beings are morally equal

---

[21] In the initial draft of the Declaration, at least Jefferson recognizes the humanity of the slaves and the criminality of slavery: "He has waged cruel war *against human nature itself, violating its most sacred rights of life and liberty in the persons* of a distant people who never offended him, captivating & carrying them into slavery in another hemisphere, or to incur miserable death in their transportation thither (my italics)."

[22] See, for example Query XVIII in his Notes on the State of Virginia. Merrill D. Peterson, ed. *Thomas Jefferson: Writings*. Washington, DC: Library of America, 1984, 289. In contemplating the immorality of slavery Jefferson writes that, "I tremble for my country when I reflect that God is just: that his justice cannot sleep forever." This does not sound like an apologist for the institution of slavery.

[23] Ibid., similarly, in Query XVIII, Jefferson's moral sense philosophy is also reflected when he expresses his hopes for the future: "The spirit of the master is abating, that of the slave rising from the dust. His condition mollifying, the way I hope preparing, under the auspices of heaven, for total emancipation."

and exist in an intrinsically social world, forced Jefferson to manage a host of moral and political contradictions as he attempted to come to grips with the controversies swirling around the issue of emancipation.[24]

We can begin to understand Jefferson's moral sense philosophy by reviewing a letter he wrote to his nephew Peter Carr (1787), a young man just beginning his university studies. Revealingly, Jefferson advises his nephew to make sure he avoids taking courses in Moral Philosophy, courses which, in his view, would be "lost time." Somewhat paradoxically, Jefferson opines to his nephew that formalized learning about moral philosophy would end up harming one's moral development. He explains why:

> He who made us would have been a pitiful bungler, if he had made the rules of our moral conduct a matter of science. For one man of science, there are thousands who are not. What would have become of them? Man was destined for society. His morality, therefore, was to be formed to this object. He was endowed with a sense of right and wrong, merely relative to this. This sense is as much a part of his nature, as the sense of hearing, seeing, feeling; it is the true foundation of morality, and not the truth as fanciful writers have imagined.[25]

When Jefferson asserts that "man was destined for society" and "his morality was formed to this object," he means to say that humans are social beings above all and that our moral capacity grows out of this *apriori* sociality. The idea that morality owed its existence to nature herself and not to the guiding hand of religious authority was revolutionary by eighteenth-century standards. In theorizing our moral capacities as something independent of religious authority, Jefferson was not only challenging the legitimacy of the most powerful institutions of the day. He was also effectively laying the social and moral foundations for a secular and enlightenment-oriented system of public education in the United States.

It is also worth noting that, from a pedagogical standpoint, Jefferson informs Carr that the type of moral sense he conceptualizes cannot be achieved through a process of implanting knowledge in young minds.

---

[24] During the so-called Missouri crisis (1820), Jefferson provides a memorable image for how he viewed the problem of slavery at that time: "We have the wolf by the ears, and we can neither hold him, nor safely let go. Justice is on one scale, and self-preservation in the other." Thomas Jefferson to John Holmes, April 22, 1820.

[25] Thomas Jefferson to Peter Carr, August 10, 1787.

Among other implications, this statement reflects Jefferson's belief that the cultivation of moral development requires a more holistic approach, one that extends far beyond learning about the canonical traditions of Moral Philosophy and their storied internal disputes. It seems that Jefferson recognizes that the education of the moral sense, precisely because it's a potential capacity, can only be "drawn-out" or "exercised," not merely filled up with pieces of "moral knowledge." He continues:

> The moral sense, or conscience, is as much a part of man as his leg or arm. It is given to all human beings in a stronger or weaker degree, as force of members is given them in a greater or lesser degree. It may be strengthened by exercise, as may any particular limb of the body. This sense is submitted, indeed, in some degree, to the guidance of reason; but that is a small stock which is required for this: even a less one than what we call common sense. State a moral case to a ploughman and a professor. The former will decide it as well, and often better than the latter, because he has not been led astray by artificial rules.[26]

That a ploughman would often decide a moral case better than a professor reveals a great deal about Jefferson's image of the human psyche. Jefferson's conceptualization of the psyche informs the whole basis of his moral sense philosophy. To further understand Jefferson's moral sense philosophy, then, we can turn to an oft-quoted letter that he penned in the 1780s.

In writing to his Parisian love interest, Maria Cosway, Jefferson orchestrates a dialogue between the Head (reason) and the Heart (the moral sense). Speaking for the Heart, Jefferson declares: "When nature assigned us the same habitation, she gave us over it a divided empire. To you she allotted the field of science; to me that of morals."[27] The notion of a *divided empire within* seems to imply for Jefferson the necessity of acknowledging the limits of the "frigid calculations" of reason and, by extension, science. This is why the ploughman (as symbolic of the heart/moral sense) would likely decide a moral case better than a professor (as symbolic of the head/reason). Jefferson suspects the professor would tend to be "led astray by artificial rules," while the farmer would

[26] Ibid.
[27] Thomas Jefferson to Maria Cosway, October 12, 1786.

tend to negotiate moral dilemmas from a more intuitive perspective—without recourse to formalized pieces of canonical knowledge. In rhetorically assuming the identity of the metaphoric Heart, Jefferson expresses the limits of the Head:

> In denying to you (Reason/Science) the feeling of sympathy, of benevolence, of gratitude, of justice, of love, of friendship, she has excluded you from their control. To these she has adapted the mechanism of the heart. Morals were too essential to the happiness of man to be risked on the uncertain combinations of the head. She laid their foundation therefore in sentiment, not in science.[28]

Here, Jefferson makes use of a conventional, if simplistic reason/emotion binary to identify six principles or virtues that signify the moral half of the "divided empire" within. In examining the human feelings (sentiments) that are commonly ascribed to the principles that Jefferson identifies—sympathy, benevolence, gratitude, justice, love, and friendship—we begin to grasp the rationale Jefferson adopts to support his belief that we are first social beings and, from this condition, emerge our moral capacities.

The theoretical inseparability between the social and moral origins of human identity are brought into clearer relief when we consider the feelings typically associated with each of these six moral virtues. Each of them, for example, elicit feelings that are fundamentally defined by their "other-directedness." Why is this so? It is so because the substantive content of the moral ideals themselves, despite other qualitative differences, each involve *a fundamental reconfiguration of the Self's relation to the Other.* Each one of these states of being, practically speaking, causes the Self to identify with the Other in a more visceral, moral fashion. Putting the same point differently, we could say that none of these moral ideals would tend to manifest themselves by persons thinking or acting in an atomized, solipsistic, or wholly self-interested manner. The realization of the moral ideals that Jefferson enumerates above involve the *exercise and activation of imaginative powers* that atomized individuals—or possessive individualists—have had diminished from their emotional inventory. It is difficult for this character type, then, to be and act in other-directed or other-regarding ways. When the imaginative capacities within this type of identity formation become atrophied through the socialization process,

[28] Ibid.

a range of possible broader identifications—from caring about others, to caring about the planet—become significantly narrowed. As Martha Nussbaum has argued, since the arts and humanities are the best, if not the only curricular traditions for exercising and cultivating our moral imaginations, to cut them out of the curriculum is to cut out the role that the schools could and should play in forming genuinely empathetic democratic citizens.[29]

Let us assume, for the moment, in line with Jefferson and the moral sense tradition, that human beings are inherently social beings whose moral capacities spring from this primal fact. The question arises how Jefferson's moral sense philosophy might be theorized to serve as a social and moral foundation for redirecting today's educational purposes.

To prepare the conceptual ground for such a creative task, perhaps it would help to first recognize that the underlying assumptions about human nature that form the basis of Jefferson's moral sense philosophy, are virtually identical to the assumptions about human nature that form the basis of Charles Darwin's interpretation of human nature. Writing contrary to conventional wisdom, David Loye brings to our attention that Darwin believed human existence is rooted in its sociality and, accordingly, we evolved a moral capacity that gives humans a transcendent, revisionary potential. In quoting Darwin below, notice how closely his interpretation of human nature aligns with the rationale that Jefferson provides for his moral sense philosophy.

> We have seen how, with the aid of active intellectual powers and the effects of habit, the social instincts—the prime principle of our moral constitution—lead over our evolution to the golden rule 'As ye would that others should do unto you, you do to them likewise.' Here lies the foundation of morality.[30]

According to Loye's trenchant analysis, a large part of the "hidden crisis" of western education lies in the fact that Darwin's deepest insights into the social and moral wellsprings of human nature continue to be

---

[29] See, Martha Nussbaum, *Not for Profit: Why Democracy Needs the Humanities.* Princeton University Press, 2008.

[30] As quoted in David Loye, "Darwin's Lost Theory and the Hidden Crisis in Western Education." In *Education for a Culture of Peace*, eds. Rianne Eisler and Ron Miller. Portsmouth, NH: Heinemann, 2004, 48.

grotesquely distorted within most American school curriculums. When curricular purposes are evaluated according to the kinds of identity formations they produce, Loye finds that human beings are defined by their essential selfishness, a meaning narrative that not coincidentally reinforces the moral legitimacy of a capitalist social imaginary. Loye contends that, while this conventional view permeates both American society and its school cultures, it's factually at odds with Darwin's view that human beings ought to be defined by their social and moral capacities for compassion.

Based on the insights into current curricular trends offered by Nussbaum and Loye, it's warranted to assert that the social and moral foundations of human existence are being systematically denied to the degree that our schools privilege a kind of possessive individualism as the tacit gold standard of human identity. Further, owing to the continued demotion of civic education and the humanities from the nation's public school curriculum, it also seems warranted to assert that the schools are increasingly complicit in ordaining the reproduction of mass idiocy.[31] In thus denying the social and moral foundations of human being itself, the neoliberal paradigm of education can be seen as denying the democratic foundations upon which education for citizenship should rest. To the degree that our increasingly privatized schools continue to produce atomized, solipsistic, and wholly self-interested cultural identity formations (as will be argued in Chapter 8), they will arguably continue to squander those types of educational opportunities and experiences that would enable the young to learn from their encounters with Others.

To clarify this key claim of an essential human relationality, Michael P. Zuckert interprets how Jefferson linked the moral and social dimensions of human being:

> We are irreducibly social in that we can (and do) enter into the feelings of others—or rather they enter into us. We "feel their pain"; we sense their pleasures. It is this faculty to which Jefferson appeals when he insists that

---

[31] To the extent the schools function to reinforce images of possessive individualism—an identity formation Wendy Brown has called *Homo Economicus*—they produce privatized individual identities: this conforms to the Greek definition of *idios* as a purely private person. The term was thus invented to describe persons who could legally participate in the polis but chose not to, a choice which Greeks disparaged because only by participating in the larger civic realm, they thought, could human beings actualize their full potential.

"nature hath implanted in our breasts" something that draws us to the good of others.[32]

In emphasizing the vital role that imagination plays in enabling the Self to identify with the feelings of Others, Zuckert affirms how crucial this faculty is to Jefferson's theory of the moral sense. Indeed, the all-important human capacity of revisability, outlined at the outset of the chapter as the basis of his revolutionary theory, is similarly dependent upon the imaginative function for the realization of its potential. In a sense, then, *to revise is to imagine beyond the given*. And in our capacity to recognize good in others, along with a receptivity to the feelings of others, our moral imaginations can become stimulated, as we (in theory) broaden the range of our social identifications. In this way, the stimulation of our moral imaginations creates added opportunities for the emergence of our capacities to revise. As I have suggested, the logic of this conceptual schema indicates why civic education and the humanities are so crucial to the project of human flourishing—as curricular traditions, they are uniquely suited for mobilizing our imaginations—particularly in relation to how we perceive the Self/Other relation, a kind of moral perception that can itself become educative and transformative.

THE MORAL SENSE AND THE SPIRIT OF 76

The passages above may remind readers of a core theme discussed in Chapter 2. If we recall, Jefferson expressed hope that there would emerge a growing generational "sentiment" and "intuition" for openness to intergenerational revolutionary change. In effect, Jefferson asserts that the Spirit of 76 is a signifier housing *moral sentiments* and *intuitions* capable of metaphorically "ripening" over time. This openness to political renewal, let us recall, was seen to be propelled by historically fresh interpretations of the moral principles at the "heart" of the Spirit of 76.

To summarize the main themes of the chapter, then, we have seen that Jefferson frames the Spirit of 76 as that which would tend to morally ripen when property relations were more or less evenly distributed, when

---

[32] See Michael P. Zuckert, "Thomas Jefferson and Natural Morality: Classical Moral Theory, Moral Sense, and Rights." In *Thomas Jefferson, the Classical World, and Early America*, eds. Peter Onuf and Nicholas Cole. Charlottesville: University of Virginia Press, 2011, 73.

knowledge and intelligence were diffused among the mass of citizens, and when citizens were simultaneously exposed, through free education and a free press, to a diversity of opinions and experiences.

In theory, then, were the nation to organize itself according to Jefferson's egalitarian structural design (a theme developed in Part II), this egalitarian structure would generate a corresponding social spirit which might itself become an educative force. In turn, the introduction of such a social dynamic into society would supply a constant impetus toward political and cultural renovation. The spiritual and philosophical idea of a permanently evolving American experiment—rooted in the cultivation of the intuitions and moral sentiments contained within the Spirit of 76—was for Jefferson the soul of the nation's revolutionary prospect.

As we ask ourselves what it would mean to restore civic purposes to the schools based on present-day needs, we confront, once again, the problem of *Homo Economicus*. This metaphoric creature, as the progeny of neoliberalism, has been deployed as a rhetorical device to describe the kind of identity formation produced when the construction of educational purposes are dominated by economic, market-driven values. It seems that what our youth need today is not a tweaking of the existing curriculum, but a radical transformation of it. That is, a transformation from a dominant economic purpose to a newly articulated moral and civic purpose. It would appear that our educational interpretation of Jefferson's revolutionary theory, when undergirded by his moral sense philosophy, could provide a theoretical foundation for igniting and guiding such a transformation of educational purpose.

CHAPTER 4

Twentieth-Century Jeffersonian Intervention: John Dewey and the Predicaments of American Democracy

Preliminary Reflections

To clarify the conceptual organization and thematic sequencing of the next two chapters, it may be useful to first restate three propositions introduced in Chapters 2 and 3 regarding Jefferson's holistic vision of education. While these propositions represent related strands of Jefferson's educational thought, when considered as a whole, they accurately describe the moral foundations of Jefferson's construction of educational purpose.

The first proposition is that Jefferson's secular faith in the capacity of human beings to succeed at the experiment in self-government was explicitly predicated on the state fulfilling its responsibility to encourage greater levels of public intelligence among the mass of citizens. The generous disposition Jefferson expresses toward "the people" with respect to his educational proposals, particularly in *caring about their general enlightenment and believing in the possibility of their enlightenment,* was said to reflect a core element of his revolutionary theory. It was further contended that Jefferson's belief in the educability of the people qualified as an expression of an underlying educational *demophilia*—particularly in contrast to the *demophobic* Hamiltonian tradition.

The second proposition is that Jefferson's theory of permanent revolution, in its dependence upon the general enlightenment of the people to supply its forward thrust, carried with it an *assumption of trust in the*

© The Author(s) 2020
K. T. Burch, *Jefferson's Revolutionary Theory and the Reconstruction of Educational Purpose,* The Cultural and Social Foundations of Education, https://doi.org/10.1007/978-3-030-45763-1_4

social and moral capacities of citizens to grow in relation to the "Spirit of '76." This spirit was described by Jefferson metaphorically as a "vestal flame" of moral virtue, while I have referred to it as a "mytho-poetic meaning narrative." Among other characteristics, this spirit can be interpreted to symbolize the principles of equality of opportunity, of liberty, of public happiness, and of developing political knowledge of one's rights, along with a readiness to defend them against domestic manifestations of ambition, corruption, tyranny. Thus, the spirit as conceived by Jefferson seemed to exist as a synthesis of several enlightenment moral ideals, representing a symbolic field of meaning that, despite its apparent magnificence, was still liable to being unlearned and forgotten by the people.

The third proposition is that Jefferson's moral sense philosophy informed his optimistic hope for the attainment of human progress. It was assumed that the moral sense tradition of the Scottish Enlightenment informed Jefferson's definition of humans as essentially moral beings and therefore as essentially good—at least *potentially*, provided, as has been emphasized, hospitable republican social and political conditions were furnished. The case was made that Jefferson's moral sense philosophical approach rejected individualistic images of identity (and happiness). Instead, it was posited that individuals should be defined in line with the assumption of human interrelationality, a perspective that transcended the reduction of one's identity to merely an economic function. It was proposed, finally, that *the Jeffersonian interpretation of human identity as something essentially social and moral provides a sound philosophical justification for constructing the public schools on the basis of a civic purpose.*

With these three propositions serving as a conceptual template for lending coherence to the moral foundations of Jefferson's revolutionary thought, we turn now to an exploration of how these and other Jeffersonian legacies were given theoretical updates in the twentieth century by two prominent and influential educational thinkers, John Dewey and George Counts.

In this chapter and in Chapter 5, I discuss how Dewey, a philosopher of education, and Counts, a sociologist of education, defined themselves in relation to the Jeffersonian tradition during decades of protracted national crisis—from the 1920s to the 1940s. There are good reasons to focus on the rhetorical uses of Jefferson during these decades, particularly during the Great Depression. It was a time when the nation's fragile democratic identity was radically imperiled and the already brutal structural inequalities between rich and poor intensified to dangerous proportions. The prospect of violent revolution emanating from the left or the right, or from both directions at once, suddenly seemed more than just a theoretical possibility. Within this stormy and uncertain political climate, it's not surprising that Jefferson might speak powerfully to Dewey and Counts as they surveyed the wreckage of a capitalist system and the seeming collapse of its corresponding cultural myth of rugged individualism.

THE JEFFERSONIAN SUBTEXT OF DEWEY'S DEMOCRATIC THEORY

In a 1936 article in *The Social Frontier*, Dewey observed that many commentators in his day (and before) had been dismissing Jefferson's vision and legacy as "outmoded."[1] This dominant historiographical narrative was grounded mainly, though not exclusively, in the notion that because Jefferson believed so fervently in the superiority of agricultural over industrial regimes to produce a virtuous citizenry, the relative decline of agriculture during the industrial age meant that the underlying rationale for Jeffersonian democracy was effectively destroyed. Dewey, however, countered that this was a "highly superficial view."[2] Here, Dewey is not disputing the fact that industrialism decimated whole ways of life and produced identities that were metaphoric light-years away from Jefferson's preferred vision of nationhood. What Dewey did dispute, however, was the conventional wisdom that Jefferson's political thought was no longer capable of generating insight into twentieth-century industrial conditions.

Dewey stresses that what Jefferson was most concerned about regarding the development of an industrial-based economic and political order, was that such a regime would magnify structural inequalities. This, in turn, would undermine the formation of intelligent, virtuous citizens, as Dewey notes: "Jefferson predicted what the effects... of an industrial regime would be, unless the independence and liberty characteristic of the farmer, under conditions of virtually free land, were conserved."[3] Dewey also seems to appreciate that Jefferson's predictions about the baneful consequences of industrialization for both American society and for the

---

[1] John Dewey, "Liberalism and Equality." *The Social Frontier*, Vol. 2, No. 4, 1936, 105–106. Quoted in *The Social Frontier: A Critical Reader*, ed. Eugene F. Provenzo, Jr. New York: Peter Lang, 2011, 150–151.

[2] Ibid., 150.

[3] Ibid.

formation of its national identity, had indeed come to pass. Yet, the rise of an industrial civilization, moving in the opposite direction of Jefferson's agricultural arcadia, was never construed by Dewey to mean that Jefferson's heuristic value had become exhausted.

Dewey makes this crucial analytical distinction: "...it was not agrarianism per se that he really stood for, but the kind of liberty and equality that the agrarian regime made possible when there was an open frontier."[4] In this rendering, Dewey articulates the organic connection between land ownership and the development of a virtuous citizenry, a central piece of Jefferson's holistic vision. So while it was undeniable that an industrial regime had supplanted an agriculture one as the dominant force in American life, Dewey insisted that Jefferson's contributions to the American political tradition retained an ability to productively interpret twentieth-century conditions.

In his endeavor to re-present the image of Jefferson in the public imagination, Dewey argues that the democratic model of national identity, which Jefferson did so much to rhetorically advance, had been distorted by the cultural power of a "so-called rugged individualism which defines the liberty of individuals in terms of the inequality bred by existing economic-legal institutions."[5] Dewey uses surprisingly sharp language to describe this economic (Hamiltonian) model of national identity. Dewey declared that the nation's existing materialism places a "blight on the cultural development of individuals." This *blight* placed on individuals—a term denoting a kind of moral disease—is described as the "inevitable product of exaggeration of the economic liberty of the few at the expense of the all-around liberty of the many."[6]

Although Dewey doesn't explicitly blame the Hamiltonian model of national identity as one of the ultimate causes of the Great Depression, he certainly appears to do so implicitly. And, just in case readers of *The Social Frontier* failed to grasp the full import of his searing indictment of the Hamiltonian model of national identity, Dewey repeats himself one

[4] Ibid.
[5] Ibid., 151.
[6] Ibid.

sentence later: "this limitation upon genuine liberty is the *inevitable product* of the inequality that arises and must arise under the operations of institutionally established and supported finance-capitalism."[7]

In these passages, Dewey interprets the Hamilton/Jefferson rhetorical trope in rigid binary terms. As we shall read in Chapter 5, this trope is similarly affirmed for its explanatory value by George Counts, whereby Counts treats what might be called the "Hamiltonian effect" on the national identity formation as constituting a major problem to overcome.

Writing a few years later, under the title *The Living Thoughts of Thomas Jefferson* (1940), Dewey offers a more nuanced theoretical treatment of the Jefferson/Hamilton trope.[8] Here, Dewey defines the conflict between the Jeffersonian and Hamiltonian models of national identity as inescapable, suggesting that it contains something of a perennial character. Because of the recurring cultural tension between these two models, Dewey wants readers to regard the tension itself as potentially educative, presumably owing to the cognitive dissonance it may engender when critically reflected upon. Dewey cautions that it would be a "great pity if partisan differences" were to "disable us from appreciating the greatness of our common American heritage." "If Jefferson was right," Dewey observes, "the source of the difference lies deep in the varying attitudes of human nature."[9] Given, then, that Jefferson and Hamilton symbolize a set of underlying philosophical divisions regarding the question of human nature, Dewey writes that his hearty endorsement of the Jeffersonian perspective was less important than the active contemplation among citizens of the tension itself.

In his book *Freedom and Culture* (1939/1989), Dewey returns to address one of the reasons why Jefferson's image had been misunderstood over the years.[10] Namely, he asserts that Jefferson's advocacy of a state's rights doctrine led many observers to overlook its democratic resonances. From a contemporary viewpoint, it's not difficult to see why this would happen.

[7] Ibid.

[8] John Dewey, *The Living Thoughts of Thomas Jefferson*. New York: Longmans, Green, 1940 (Subsequent references to this text will be noted as, *LTTJ*).

[9] Ibid., 3.

[10] John Dewey, "Democracy and America." In *Freedom and Culture*. Buffalo, NY: Prometheus Books, 1939/1989, 121.

DEWEY'S REPRESENTATION
OF JEFFERSON'S DEMOCRATIC FAITH

As was the case in the previous section, it is important to bear in mind
the historical context within which Dewey interprets Jefferson's legacy.
Dewey does not decide to take-up Jefferson's legacy in the 1890s, in the
early 1900s, or even in the 1920s. Nor does Jefferson's name appear in
any of Dewey's major works, such as *Democracy and Education* (1916),
Reconstruction in Philosophy (1920), and *The Public and Its Problems*
(1926). Dewey only decides to focus his critical attention on Jefferson in
the depths of the Great Depression and on the precipice of World War II
(1939–1940). Why, then, does Jefferson become a focal point for Dewey
at this specific moment?

According to rhetorical theorist Jeremy Engels, Dewey came belat-
edly to Jefferson in the late thirties once he realized that another global
war was inevitable.[18] Engels contends that Dewey foresaw the reactionary
domestic effects that would likely be part of post-World War II America
(think McCarthyism). By the late 1930s, Dewey was thus ready to recruit
Jefferson as a resource to help him think through a more robust democratic response to the anti-democratic tendencies that he anticipated—
correctly, it turns out—would dominate American political culture after
the war.

Tellingly, when Dewey updates Jefferson's legacy in his book *Freedom and Culture* (1939), the first thing he does is apologize to readers for "concerning himself unduly with the English writers who have
attempted to state the ideals of self-governing communities and the methods appropriate to their realization."[19] Dewey says he now values Jefferson more than ever because he realizes that Jefferson's democratic doctrine is "moral through and through: in its foundations, its methods, its
ends." Dewey adds approvingly: 'The heart of his faith is expressed in
the words "Nothing in unchangeable but the inherent and inalienable
rights of man."'[20] Dewey declares that few could describe as thoroughly

---

[18] Jeremy Engels, "Dewey on Jefferson: Reiterating Democratic Faith in Times of War."
In *Trained Capacities: John Dewey, Rhetoric, and Democratic Practice*, eds. Brian Jackson
and Gregory Clark. Columbia: University of South Carolina Press, 2014, 88–89.

[19] Dewey, *Freedom and Culture*, 119.

[20] Ibid.

and intimately as Jefferson the definitions and axioms of a free government. Yet, despite Jefferson's eloquence in expressing the principles of self-government, Dewey reports the sobering reality that, "the words in which he stated the moral basis of free institutions have gone out of vogue."[21] He laments that "we repeat the opening words of the Declaration of Independence, but unless we translate them they are couched in a language that, even when it comes readily to our tongue, does not penetrate today to the brain."

Dewey is sensitive to the fact that our interpretations of the country's founding documents would shift and evolve, so that words, concepts, symbols, and truths once deemed "self-evident" and "revolutionary" to one generation, would almost inevitably become less so to future generations. As we have seen, a key element of Jefferson's theory of revolution is the recognition that the original spirit and meaning of the revolutionary event will, in varying degrees, recede from public consciousness until its discourse, symbols, and myths, become an ever dimmer memory, no longer able to "penetrate to the brain." The tendency for revolutionary ideas to lose their metaphoric steam over time represents both a sobering fact and a pedagogical challenge of the highest order.

It has been stated in previous chapters that one of the positive features of Jefferson's theory of permanent revolution is that it encourages us to think more perceptively about what it might mean to breathe new life into the moral precepts of the American Revolution. Both Jefferson and Dewey, albeit from different historical locations, place this foundational civic challenge on our pedagogical radar.

While the task of reinterpreting this mythopoetic field of meaning is doubtless problematic on all fronts, Dewey nonetheless seems to believe that the revolutionary moral content of that elusive spirit was identifiable and pedagogically salvageable. To begin the process of rethinking the meaning of this spirit in a twentieth- century context, Dewey highlights what he takes to be the moral and methodological substance of Jefferson's legacy:

> ...it was the *ends* of democracy, the rights of *man*—not of men in the plural—which are unchangeable. It was not the forms and mechanisms

[21] Ibid.

through which inherent moral claims are realized that are to persist without change.[22]

Dewey is correct here. Jefferson was emphatic that it was the "forms and mechanisms" of a democratic republic that *had to change* if they were to be renewed as instruments to advance the unchangeable rights of humankind. Indeed, the whole edifice of Jefferson's theory of permanent revolution was predicated on the distinction between what *never* changes (human rights) and those things that *must* change (institutional forms and mechanisms).

Dewey demonstrates the practical import of this theoretical distinction by focusing on one of the most intractable moral predicaments facing the nation's democratic prospect. That is, the tendency among too many Americans to reduce the meaning of democracy to nothing more than an external institution embodied by the state (i.e., as an unchanging form or mechanism). Dewey argued that, to the extent democracy was interpreted as something located exclusively outside the individual, and to the extent its meanings were symbolically divorced from the personal attitudes and dispositions of individuals, democracy as a living ideal would inevitably become overly mechanized and thus drained of moral content.

Today, this deep-seated cultural bias continues to have the effect of preventing individuals from recognizing democracy in a broader cultural sense. That is, democracy conceived as a form of "moral and spiritual association," consisting of a set of values and social dispositions that are "moral through and through."[23]

In concretizing one example of how popular images of democracy can be mechanized and stripped of personal moral substance, Dewey remarks that "the most flagrant violation of Jefferson's democratic point of view is found in the widespread idolatry of the U.S. Constitution."[24] Such idolatry of external forms and mechanisms, such as the Constitution and the Pledge of Allegiance, comes at the expense of knowing the spiritual and moral dimensions of democracy. This common sense cultural pattern—a fatal misreading of what democracy is—signifies one of the ways in which democracy is commonly eviscerated.

---

[22] Ibid., 120.
[23] Ibid., 119.
[24] Ibid., 121.

Echoing, then, a specific strand of Jefferson's revolutionary theory, Dewey declares that Americans have a "right and duty to question" existing mechanisms and forms (he specifically cites the country's voting procedures as something requiring change).[25] Jefferson and Dewey thus share a rather significant epistemic bias, insofar as they define the meaning of democracy in explicitly moral, experimental, educational, and evolutionary terms—and not simply as an already finished external structure.

DEWEY'S EXTENSION OF JEFFERSON'S *DEMOPHILIA*

In his *LTTJ* essay, Dewey asserts that Jefferson's trust in the people constitutes the core moral foundation of his political and educational philosophy. This moral premise of trust or faith in the people (Dewey uses both terms interchangeably) explains why Jefferson could believe in the notion of human educability. He trusted that, given the proper opportunities, people were capable of both governing themselves and in transforming themselves through education (education understood in its broad cultural sense). According to Dewey, this foundational trust led Jefferson to the corollary proposition that "the only legitimate object of government is to secure the greatest degree of happiness possible to the general mass associated under it."[26] Below, Dewey refers to the ideological conflict between Hamilton and Jefferson over the question of human nature:

> I am not underestimating Jefferson's abilities as a practical politician when I say that this deep-seated faith in the people and their responsiveness to enlightenment properly presented was a most important factor in enabling him to effect, against great odds, "the revolution of 1800." It is the cardinal element bequeathed by Jefferson to the American tradition.[27]

Dewey's formulation here well describes a moral cornerstone of Jefferson's revolutionary theory, which, among other things, rests on the people's receptivity to psychological and civic growth (the capacity to revise). For Dewey, then, the most extraordinary feature of the "revolution of 1800," (a presidential election that Jefferson narrowly won) is

[25] Ibid.
[26] *LTTJ*, 17.
[27] Ibid., 18.

reflected in the faith Jefferson had in the people's ability to revise themselves and choose an alternative future through intelligent civic action. That the people could achieve such a feat after twelve years of elite-Federalist rule, vindicated Jefferson's enlightenment assumptions. In Jefferson's view, the people had staged an epic political course reversal—against an elite-aristocratic form of government and in favor of a democratic form—choosing a Jeffersonian vision of nationhood over a Hamiltonian vision.[28]

Dewey writes that the implications of Jefferson's baseline assumptions about the defining elements of human nature, led to his belief that the ultimate powers of political society must be lodged with the people. Such a moral stance, in turn, necessitated a corresponding commitment to their progressive enlightenment. Below, Dewey refers to the ideological conflict between Hamilton and Jefferson over the question of human nature:

> The will of the people as the moral basis of government and the happiness of the people as its controlling aim were so firmly established with Jefferson that it was axiomatic that the only alternative to the republican position was fear, in lieu of trust, of the people.[29]

Arguably, it was this tension—whether to trust or to fear the people, whether to educate them or not—that marked the symbolic dividing line between the two major political parties in the early republic. As if to undermine the nervous concerns of the self-identified *demophobic* Hamiltonians, Jefferson retorts: "...and if we think them not enlightened enough to exercise their control with a wholesome discretion, the remedy is not to take power away from the people, but to inform their discretion through education."[30]

Jefferson's historically innovative remedies for informing the discretion of citizens, however, were never convincing to the Hamiltonians, whose

---

[28] The following two authors tend to corroborate Jefferson's own interpretation: Michael A. Bellesiles, "'The Soil Will Be Soaked in Blood': Taking the Revolution of 1800 Seriously." In *The Revolution of 1800*, eds. James Horn, Jan Ellen Lewis and Peter Onuf. Charlottesville: University of Virginia Press, 2002, 59–86; Dan Sisson, *The Revolution of 1800: How Jefferson Rescued Democracy from Tyranny and Faction—And What It Means Today*. Berrett-Koehler, 2013.

[29] *LTTJ*, 17.

[30] Thomas Jefferson to William Charles Jarvis, September, 28, 1820.

operative assumption was that the majority of citizens were uneducable. The Hamiltonians believed that ordinary people could not govern themselves and could not learn to govern themselves. On the basis of these rather dreary assumptions regarding human possibility, it would follow that "the people" must be feared and controlled.[31]

When we consider the Hamiltonian definition of human nature in juxtaposition to the Jeffersonian, it seems justified to claim (taking note of previous caveats) that Jefferson's political and educational philosophy is rooted in an underlying *demophilia*. We see Dewey exemplify this preference throughout his long career, especially in those writings where he spotlights the reproductive linkages between democracy and the moral identity of the nation. The Jeffersonian subtext of Dewey's democratic theory, for example, is both reflected and extended in this definitive passage:

> Democracy is a way of life controlled by a faith in the possibilities of human nature. Belief in the Common Man is a familiar article in the democratic creed. That belief is without basis and significance save as it means faith in the potentialities of human nature as that nature is exhibited in every human being irrespective of race, color, sex, birth and family, of material or cultural wealth. This faith may be enacted in statutes, but it is only on paper unless it is put in force in the attitudes that human beings display to one another in all the incidents and relations of daily life.[32]

Similar to Jefferson, Dewey is clear in his belief in the possibilities of human nature, a belief that brings with it the imperative of the state and national governments to provide the proper material and social conditions that would enable these capacities to reach fulfillment.

> Democracy is a way of personal life controlled not merely by faith in human nature in general but by faith in the capacity of human beings for intelligent judgment and action if proper conditions are furnished.[33]

[31] See, for example, Jeremy Engels, "Demophilia: A Discursive Counter to Demophobia in the Early Republic." *Quarterly Journal of Speech*, Vol. 97, No. 2, May 2011, 131–154.

[32] John Dewey, "Creative Democracy—The Task Before Us." In *The Essential Dewey: Volume 1: Pragmatism, Education, Democracy*, eds. Larry A. Hickman and Thomas M. Alexander. Bloomington, IN: Indiana University Press, 1998, 343.

[33] Ibid., 342.

For both thinkers, democratic republics had an objective interest in furnishing such hospitable conditions, such as free and equal public schools, to help foster the development of an alert citizenry. These types of public policies—taken on behalf of the people's interest—would seem to qualify as a "loving action," in that it requires a profound faith and trust in the capacity of ordinary people to revise themselves both individually and in relation to others.

For all of these reasons, perhaps we should not be surprised that Dewey's interpretation of what constitutes the essence of democracy beautifully mirrors the essence of Jefferson's revolutionary theory:

> The very idea of democracy, the meaning of democracy, must be continually explored afresh; it has to be constantly discovered, and rediscovered, remade and reorganized; while the political and economic and social institutions in which it is embodied have to be remade and reorganized to meet the changes that are going on in the development of new needs on the part of human beings and new resources for satisfying these needs.[34]

For Dewey, then, as for Jefferson, the ultimate challenge that democracy poses to education is the creation of individuals and cultures capable of such political and cultural inventiveness. Since the development of new needs on the part of human beings is inevitable, the only remaining question is whether individuals and cultures will learn to be responsive to those evolving needs. The question of what it would mean to rethink and renew our public school curriculums in such a way that they could respond to the needs of a new generation of Americans, is a subject taken up in Chapters 10 and 11.

[34] John Dewey, "The Challenge of Democracy to Education." In *The Later Works, 1925–1953*, Vol. 11, ed. Jo Ann Boydston. Carbondale, IL: Southern Illinois University Press, 1987, 182.

CHAPTER 5

Reading George Counts's "A Call to the Teachers of the Nation" as a Jeffersonian Text

Retrieving the Image of Jefferson in Hard Times

One of the most fascinating yet least heralded educational texts to emerge from the Depression years was George S. Counts's 1933 pamphlet, *A Call to the Teachers of the Nation.*[1] Today, it's usually overlooked among teachers in the social foundations of education in favor of his better-known book, published in 1932, *Dare the Schools Build a New Social Order?*[2] While the two manifestos share many of the same features, notably an admonition to the teachers of the nation to awaken to their historic task of reconstructing American democracy, they differ in one critical respect. *A Call* provides a valuable historical analysis of the nation's political tradition that's not found in *Dare the Schools*; thus, *A Call* highlights Jefferson's role as the ideological architect of what Counts calls the "democratic-revolutionary tradition," while *Dare the Schools* simply isn't designed to treat Jefferson or the American political tradition more generally.

[1] George S. Counts, *A Call to the Teachers of the Nation.* New York: John Day Co., 1933. All subsequent references to this text will be cited as *A Call.*

[2] George S. Counts, *Dare the Schools Build a New Social Order?* Carbondale: Southern Illinois University, 1932. All subsequent references to this text will be cited as *Dare the Schools.*

© The Author(s) 2020   71
K. T. Burch, *Jefferson's Revolutionary Theory and the Reconstruction of Educational Purpose*, The Cultural and Social Foundations of Education, https://doi.org/10.1007/978-3-030-45763-1_5

The inclusion of this historical dimension is significant. It permits Counts to integrate into his analysis what is perhaps the most foundational contradiction animating the trajectory of US history: the conflict between what he calls the "democratic-revolutionary tradition" and the "elite-aristocratic tradition."[3] As we have seen, this conflict reflects divergent interpretations of human nature and of the human prospect itself. In surveying the controversies brought about by the breakdown of an elite-driven class structure during the Great Depression, Counts declared that American society had entered a "revolutionary epoch" in which the culture "is already at war with itself."[4] Meanwhile, his ally John Dewey, evaluating the same economic, political, and cultural breakdowns, similarly observed that, in terms of economic class, "we are a house divided against itself, our tradition, our heritage, is itself double."[5]

It was, then, the democratic-revolutionary tradition symbolized by Jefferson's writings that Counts believed had to be imaginatively retrieved for the nation's democracy to genuinely reconstruct itself. Counts understands that this tradition, and its laudable moral ideals, arose in a historical context that, in most ways, no longer existed. For both thinkers, the growing disjuncture between the ideals of American democracy and its undemocratic realities, was recognized as a fact of the utmost importance. It was taken by both thinkers as a kind of theoretical scaffolding for the project of breathing new life into the revolutionary democratic tradition, but now in the context of an industrial civilization. As Counts put it, "the situation calls for a reinterpretation of the great ideal…if democracy is to survive, it must be divorced from its union with the simple agrarian life of the past and be readjusted to the complex industrial society of the present."[6] "If its spirit is to live on," Counts added, "its forms must suffer radical change."[7] Both Dewey and Counts wanted to engage the task of reconstructing American democracy by making an analytical distinction between the *spirit* of the ideal, on the one hand, and the myriad

[3] *A Call*, 13.

[4] Ibid., 16.

[5] John Dewey, "A House Divided Against Itself." In *Individualism Old and New*. Buffalo, NY: Prometheus Books, 1999, 5–9.

[6] *A Call*, 17.

[7] Ibid.

forms within which that spirit had been historically sequestered, directed, corralled, disciplined and, on occasion, positively ignited.

The aim of attaining a better understanding of the dialectical relationship that exists between the spirit (as a living moral substance) and the form (constitutional mechanisms) occupies a central place within Dewey's and Count's theory of American democracy. Both thinkers focus attention on the conflicts and contradictions contained within the nation's dual, conflicted heritage: these analyses' theorized the zones of conflict between the nation's democratic ideals and its frequently less than democratic economic and social realities. Their concerns about how to conceptually frame this dialectical relation also looms large within Jefferson's theory of permanent revolution. As we recall, the following questions were explicit within Jefferson's revolutionary theory, broadly constructed: How to retrieve the memory of the democratic moral spirit as a precondition for renewing its meaning in historically novel circumstances? How to redirect and reinvent those existing forms, laws, and mechanisms deemed incapable of promoting its revolutionary spirit?

From Individualism (Frontier Nation) to Individuality (Industrial Nation): Counts on the Democratization of American Identity

For Counts, the most significant change required to democratize the national identity during the Depression period was straightforward. It was for the American people to reject the "economic model of individualism" which functioned as the conceptual anchor of the dominant Hamiltonian paradigm.[8] Dewey, as we saw in the previous chapter, gestured toward reconciling the Hamiltonian and Jeffersonian paradigms of national identity in his suggestion that their competing legacies comprised part of a valuable national tradition. In stark contrast, Counts shows little interest in seeing anything positive in the "elite-aristocratic" Hamiltonian tradition. Much more explicitly than Dewey, Counts attempts to deconstruct Hamilton's ideology from a democratic, or Jeffersonian, perspective, and seeks to make meaning out of juxtaposing Hamilton's political philosophy alongside Jefferson's.

---

[8] Ibid., 14.

Counts not only claims that the Hamiltonian model of civic identity represented an obsolete set of ideals that should be abandoned, he implies that this identity formation played a determinative role as an underlying cause of the Great Depression.[9] He excoriates Hamilton, just as Jefferson did before him, as the leading symbol of an elite-aristocratic power bloc whose policies (and assumptions about human possibility) came to be embodied within certain constitutional forms and mechanisms that served to vitiate the democratic–republican spirit. Counts's critical analysis of what might be called the "Hamiltonian effect" on the trajectory of US history and identity is worth pausing over. Counts's interpretation mirror familiar Jeffersonian indictments of Hamiltonianism. But what's most important to note, in my opinion, is that Counts theoretically extends these indictments into fresh historical territory, so to speak, as he attempts to expose the elite-aristocratic influences which he still believed were decisively misshaping and suppressing the nation's democratic potential.

Counts begins by linking the origins of the nation's imagined identity to the prior geographical fact of the frontier experience.

> Although we have never had a clear conception of our destiny as a people and have never agreed upon the ends of living, in earlier periods the need for a common goal was much less urgent. With a scattered population and with boundless resources to the west, the ideal of rugged individualism, which can scarcely be called a social ideal because of its practical denial of social purpose, met the needs of the American people fairly well. For the most part, life was a struggle between the individual or family and nature. Under such conditions the ideal in economy of "each man for himself and the devil take the hindmost" served to release human energy on a generous scale and to hasten the physical conquest of the continent, even though it was attended by a reckless waste of irreplaceable raw materials and the development of a certain degree of callousness toward the misfortunes and sufferings of the weak and unsuccessful.[10]

Here, Counts historicizes the ideal of rugged individualism in order to explain why it was accompanied by a "practical denial of social purpose."

---

[9] Ibid.
[10] Ibid., 12.

He reminds us that this character formation grew out of frontier conditions in which there was no compelling need for citizens to have a consciously developed sense of social purpose. The very idea of developing such a common goal and social purpose to "guide the ends of living," was an idea for American citizenship whose time had not yet ripened in historical terms. For Counts as well as for Dewey, however, the question was not if objective conditions had changed sufficiently to merit a moral renovation of the national identity. Of course they had! The questions they posed, rather, revolved around how best to expose the limitations of this inherited identity formation now that the industrial age had rendered it functionally obsolete.

They sought to rearticulate and bring into being, through multiple agencies of education, a socially oriented identity formation more in line with the requirements of a democratized industrial order. At stake for Counts (and Dewey) was whether the nation would respond to the catastrophe of the Depression by maintaining the same *asocial* or *atomized* and increasingly dysfunctional form of national identity (e.g., possessive individualism), or whether the radical flux of the historical moment would be used to catalyze the development of new models of human identity. The progressive evolution of a new model of individuality is what Counts and Dewey both wanted to emerge, phoenix-like, from underneath the rubble of a collapsed economic and social order.

It is also important to emphasize the last clause of the passage cited above, because here Counts identifies a vital causal relation between the frontier experience and the formation of a morally problematic psychological disposition. This disposition is described as a "callousness toward the misfortunes and suffering of the weak and unsuccessful." No one would argue of course that callousness as a personality trait, as an attitude toward the world, would stand as a hallmark of democratic culture. In making the connection between the frontier experience and the development of a kind of moral disregard for the feelings of others, Counts's conjecture would be reinforced decades later by contemporary scholars of the frontier, such as Richard Slotkin and Richard Drinnon.[11] They

---

[11] See Richard Slotkin, *The Fatal Environment: The Myth of the Frontier in the Age of Industrialization, 1800–1890.* New York, NY: Atheneum, 1985; Richard Drinnon, *Facing West: The Metaphysics of Indian-Hating and Empire-Building.* Minneapolis: University of Minnesota Press, 1997.

persuasively show how the Self/Other difference was made more hierarchical, and more violent, through the asymmetrical power relations which governed the waves of fateful encounters between the western settlers and the indigenous people of the continent.

This encounter, however, carried implications not just for the relationship between the powerful and the indigenous people of the continent, or for anyone else defined as "less than" within the Hamiltonian imaginary. Counts's reference to the "reckless waste of irreplaceable raw materials," a practice enabled by an emotional attitude of "callousness" toward the environment, reminds us that humans must always construct an imagined relationship between themselves and the world, earth, and universe. Counts understands that callousness, as an epistemic lens on the world, is an attitude not merely confined to inter-human relations. Perhaps more ominously, this culturally constructed attitude can also be writ large, so to speak, and used as a template to define a whole set of relations between self and world.

One of Counts's foundational claims, expressed both in *A Call* and in *Prospects for Democracy* (1939), is this: The concept of a Common Good, of a social covenant, a social contract, or any other signifier representing what Counts calls a "community of purpose," is impossible to enact within the rugged individualism model of national identity. In the context of the twentieth century, Counts concludes, "today the individual can only be guaranteed freedom for cultural and spiritual growth only by the abandonment of economic individualism."[12]

According to Counts, the myth of rugged individualism—and the denial of human interrelationality it represents—was rooted primarily but not exclusively in geography. It constituted one dimension of the cultural crisis of the 1930s. But Counts identifies another, more ideologically grounded dimension of the problem:

> The situation, however, is complicated by certain other ideals which were generated in the course of our history and which are in irreconcilable conflict today. Particular reference is made to those bodies of social doctrine with which the names of Jefferson and Hamilton are commonly associated. The first may be called democratic, the second the aristocratic tradition in

---

[12] *A Call*, 17.

America; the one would make paramount the general welfare of the people, the other would organize the state about the interests of a privileged class.[13]

The Jefferson/Hamilton rhetorical trope figures prominently within Counts's analysis of American society. Counts assumed, I think correctly, that the Jefferson/Hamilton binary still retained an uncanny ability to render intelligible what *had* happened in the country, and what *could* happen in the future given the unfinished character of its democratic-revolutionary tradition.[14] For our purposes, it isn't so much Counts's theoretical acumen in recounting the historical basis of this defining ideological binary opposition that's most interesting. What's most interesting is to examine how Counts applies the trope in the 1930s to interpret the underlying dynamics of the nation's political culture, and specifically, how he used it to reveal how capitalism functioned to contradict the nation's putative commitment to democracy.

COUNTS'S CRITIQUE OF HAMILTON'S *DEMOPHOBIA*

A conspicuous feature of Counts's *A Call* is the amount of space he devotes to a critical treatment of Hamilton's elite-aristocratic ideology. Count's placed the Hamiltonian tradition in his theoretical crosshairs because, in his view, it embodied, theoretically and practically, the main educational and civic problem inhibiting the progressive development of American society and culture. It was exactly this historically continuous power bloc within the American negotiation of identity that still functioned as the nation's ideological hegemon. Its truths, myths, and symbols, including its anti-democratic discourse regarding the human prospect, had become internalized as common sense by all too many Americans, at least according to Counts's interpretation. Counts seems to be warning the Americans of his day, behold—*Homo Economicus*!

---

[13] Ibid., 12.

[14] Over the years, this rhetorical trope has seen its symbolic currency wax and wane as a tool of critical analysis. And while some have regarded it as *passe*, and no longer explanatory of the American scene, I disagree. If, for example, the Jefferson/Hamilton binary can be interpreted reductively to signify the conflict between the elite-aristocratic and democratic cultural forces operating within the negotiation of national identity, then I believe its hermeneutic value is potentially more explanatory today than ever.

Counts's describes Hamilton as one of the "first great prophets of modern capitalism in America."[15] He identifies the economic doctrine of laissez-faire capitalism championed by Hamilton as one of the underlying causes of the Great Depression. Sounding very much like Jefferson himself, Counts declared that the Hamiltonian strand of the national identity had encouraged too much power being placed in the hands of the few, without providing limits on the power of corporations and on the centrality of the profit motive.

"Unlike Jefferson," Counts observes, "Hamilton had no faith in and little regard for the common man." Counts goes directly to Hamilton's unvarnished *demophobia* and quotes him: "The people! The people is a great beast."[16] In much the same vein, Counts cites a long passage from Hamilton in which he speaks positively about the virtues of child labor as a means for increasing profit and making use of "persons who would otherwise be idle."[17]

Counts includes another passage from Hamilton that reflects his strong aversion to both democracy and to the very prospect of educating human potential:

> All communities divide themselves into the few and many. The first are the rich and well-born, the other the mass of people. The voice of the people has been said to be the voice of God; and, however generally this maxim has been quoted and believed, it is not true in fact. The people are turbulent and changing; they seldom judge or determine aright. Give, therefore, the first class a distinct, permanent share in the government.[18]

Obviously, Counts turns to Hamilton not to celebrate his legacy, but to make plain that Hamilton's ideology had "achieved triumph and remains practically unshaken down to the present time."[19] Nor was Counts particularly sanguine about the ability of the Roosevelt administration and its New Deal policies to significantly alter the nation's power structure. "It

---

[15] *A Call*, 13–16.
[16] Ibid.
[17] Ibid.
[18] Ibid., 13–14.
[19] Ibid., 14.

scarcely seems likely" he lamented, "that the present Democratic administration will actually succeed in driving the money changers out of the halls of national government. They have been there too long."[20]

It is noteworthy that Counts traces this political and ideological triumph to a late nineteenth-century US Supreme Court case (1886 *Santa Clara County v. Union Pacific Railway*). The case symbolized for Counts the capitalist/corporate triumph of the few over the many. He discusses how *Santa Clara* came to serve as the legal mechanism by which corporations were recognized as "persons," therefore investing fictional persons with the same rights as actual persons under the 14th Amendment's equal protection clause. Corporations as rights-bearing persons were now able to invoke the equal protection clause to avoid complying with laws that might impede their exercise of power. On a note of cruel irony, Counts informs us that, at the same time the original purpose of the 14th Amendment was being systematically stripped away from the newly freed, making their rights as citizens an empty farce, corporations had succeeded in appropriating one of the democratic fruits of the Civil War to further consolidate their power within the American polity. As a twentieth-century Jeffersonian public intellectual, Counts could never countenance the elevation of corporations to the status of citizens. To normalize this principle would be to nullify the ostensibly exceptional character of the American experiment, an experiment whose moral legitimacy was premised on the elevation of human rights over property rights, not the other way around. With this decision, Counts writes, the union of private industry and government was "written into the fundamental law of the land."[21] In Chapter 7, the contemporary doctrine of corporate personhood, which stems largely from this contested judicial precedent, will be the subject of a twenty-first century Jeffersonian critique.

The collapse of the capitalist economy in the United States during the 1930s moved Counts, along with Dewey, toward a greater appreciation of the role Jefferson might still play in the task of reconstructing American democracy. 'Jefferson had deep regard for the common man of his day, placed his confidence in the will of the people, scorned the pretensions of the privileged classes, and favored a rebellion at least once every twenty

---

[20] Ibid.
[21] Ibid.

years to "refresh the tree of liberty.""[22] In short, Counts frames Jefferson's *demophilia* as the driving moral force informing the democratic-revolutionary tradition.

Similar to Dewey, then, Counts anchors his vision of the democratic project in the Declaration of Independence, contending that its message of equality is capable of being perpetually relevant so long as the meaning of our democratic-revolutionary tradition remained subject to a process of constant creative reinterpretation. In a sense, "the call" that Counts issues to the teachers of the nation is a call for them to boldly engage in the process of creative reinterpretation of these first principles of American democracy, both inside and outside the schools. In the Declaration, Counts points out that Jefferson "repudiates the doctrine of the ruling class of the time that the central responsibility of the state is the protection of property interests."[23] Counts interprets the Jeffersonian tradition to mean that "the great objects of government, it proclaims to the twentieth no less than the eighteenth century are the securing of 'life, liberty, and the pursuit of happiness.'" And finally, Counts sums up: "Here is the mighty expression of the democratic ideal that should serve again and again to encourage the overthrow of entrenched privilege."[24] In emphasizing that the underlying spirit of the Declaration should serve repeatedly to encourage the overthrow of entrenched privilege, Counts describes a kind of moral impulse and outlook that clearly represents a twentieth-century extension of Jefferson's democratic telos of permanent revolution.

The Denial of Political Knowledge and the Tradition of Dissent: Counts's Jeffersonian-Inspired Critique of Teacher Identity

One of the signature qualities of both *The Call* and *Dare the Schools* is Counts's forceful admonition to the nation's teachers to wake up to their historic task of participating far more boldly than they have in the reconstruction of American democracy. As has been suggested, a large part of this awakening among teachers had to do with their need to promote a set

[22] Ibid., 12.
[23] Ibid., 12–13.
[24] Ibid., 13.

of values and purposes in synch with the democratic-revolutionary tradition. Counts dared teachers to transform their self-conceptions and vocational identities from an unconscious loyalty to a set of elite educational values and purposes, toward a conscious loyalty to a set of democratic values and purposes. Perhaps his committed opposition to entrenched privilege, his visits to the Soviet Union, and his desire to raise the consciousness of teachers explains why the federal government surveilled Counts for almost thirty years, eventually compiling a dossier that numbered 199 pages.[25]

For Counts and Dewey, the ultimate meaning of civic education was not found in memorizing the workings of beautiful mechanical structures, nor in dutifully reciting pledges of allegiance to the nation-state. These de facto forms of elitist education were not designed to promote the democratic values or to shape the development of human personality in line with those values. This type of education, one that promoted a mechanical or thin conception of democracy, absent the substance of its moral and spiritual values, was for Counts not a politically "neutral" education, even if it masqueraded as one.

The desired end goal of civic education in the United States, as it is reflected in the theories of Jefferson, Dewey, and Counts, could only be realized if the young were encouraged to critically interpret the meaning of the Spirit of 76 in always evolving historical contexts. The focus for teachers would therefore have to shift toward a greater understanding and appreciation of the values and purposes that reside within this mythopoetic field of symbolic meaning (or, potential meaning). Counts cautions us that it would be absurd for educators to present to their students these praiseworthy ideals in the abstract, detached from existing historical conditions, "for life in a world that does not exist:"

> To teach the ideal in its historic form, without the illumination that comes from an effort to apply it to contemporary society, is an extreme instance

---

[25] As part of my research into Counts, I filed a Freedom of Information (FOIA) request and have in my possession his FBI file. FOIPA Request No. 1150922-000, Counts, S. George (1930–1959). The FBI had concluded its surveillance of Counts in 1959, fifteen years before his death in 1974. The suspicion that Counts was a communist was proven baseless by the FBI as early as the 1930s, yet they continued to monitor his activities for decades.

of intellectual dishonesty. Teachers therefore cannot evade the responsibility of participating actively in the task of reconstituting the democratic
tradition and of thus working positively toward a new society.[26]

A central component of Counts's call is his constant reminders to
teachers about whose interests they should—and should not—be representing. The pages of *A Call* are replete with urgent pleas to teachers
to understand that their loyalty "goes to the great body of the laboring
population...they must always place their faith, their intelligence, their
idealistic fervor, and not merely their professional skill, at the service of
the masses of the people."[27] We may surmise from these repeated pleas,
of course, that in the decades preceding the Depression, Counts believed
that too many teachers had failed to develop a consciousness of their loyalty to the democratic tradition and, by extension, to the general welfare
of the people.

Recognizing the anti-democratic consequences of this historical pattern, Counts sought to contribute to the reconstruction of American
democracy by transforming the vocational identity of teachers:

> If the teachers are to play a positive and creative role in building a better
> social order, indeed if they are not to march in the ranks of economic,
> political, and cultural reaction, they will have to emancipate themselves
> completely from the domination of the business interests of the nation,
> cease cultivating the manners and associations of bankers and promotion
> agents, repudiate utterly the ideal of material success as the goal of edu-
> cation, acquire a realistic understanding of the forces that actually rule the
> world, and formulate a fundamental program of thought and action that
> will deal honestly and intelligently with the problems of industrial civiliza-
> tion.[28]

Notice how Counts makes use of the term *emancipate*. By invoking this
image, Counts seems to be suggesting that teachers were laboring under a
state of mental slavery, their identities effectively "incarcerated" within the
discourse and symbols of the nation's business interests. In a sense, then,

---

[26] *A Call*, 19.
[27] Ibid., 20.
[28] Ibid.

teachers seemed to have accepted President Calvin Coolidge's pithy apho-
rism spoken in the 1920s that, indeed, "the business of America is business."[29]

A defining element of the educational commitments of both Counts
and Dewey was to promote the idea among teachers that the business of
America was really democracy. Counts tells us that a crucial first step for
remedying the ongoing Hamiltonian effect among teachers would be for
teacher training programs to scrutinize the ideal of material success as a
guiding purpose of education. Counts would be happy to recognize that
today few aspiring teachers are enchanted by the lure of material success.
Counts probably makes this suggestion in a broader sense to spotlight
the contradictions that this materialistic set of ideals would always pose to
members of a self-identified democratic culture.

Another remedy Counts proffered was deeply political: for teachers to
acquire a better grasp of the political and economic forces that "actually
rule the world," as he puts it.[30] Counts's assertion that there are forces
that "actually" rule the world as opposed to, say, illusions about who or
what rules the world, has significant implications for understanding a cardinal principle of democratic political education. It underscores the point
that one of the main purposes of a democratic form of education is to
foster in citizens the capacity to make "critical" distinctions, that is, to
learn how to judge and to choose between competing values and interpretations.[31] To learn to choose between what's true and what's false,
between official disinformation and fact-based information, between fake
news and real news.

These examples suggest why the faculty of critical thinking—we could
also call it *doing* philosophy—is conceptually and practically wedded to
democracy at the deepest levels of analysis. The ontological relationship
between democracy and philosophy, as two braided modes of being, is
affirmed when Counts articulates how the development of a critical kind
of political knowledge is necessary to the survival of American democracy.
He observes that because the ideals of democracy are so firmly rooted in

---

[29] For a fuller discussion of the phrase, including its pedagogical potential for
democratic-minded teachers today, see Kerry Burch, "The Business of America Is Business." In *Democratic Transformations: Eight Conflicts in the Negotiation of American
Identity.* New York: Bloomsbury, 2012, 93–113.

[30] *A Call*, 20.

[31] The etymology of "critical" (*kritikos*) means "to judge and to choose, to make
distinctions." See, *The Barnhart Concise Dictionary of Etymology*, ed. Robert Barnhart.
New York, NY: HarperCollins, 1995, 173.

American culture, "any *undisguised* effort to place power in the hands of a small favored class would encounter the most implacable opposition"[32] (Counts's italics).

For Counts, then, given the already established, yet still fragile democratic sensibilities of the American people, any efforts to advance elite power would have to be *disguised* or re-packaged as a pro-democratic appeal. Following Counts's interpretation, we are invited to envision an image of a profoundly anti-democratic political figure who nonetheless poses as a friend of the people. Sound familiar? Counts speculates, based on the fascist resurgence in the 1930s, that if indeed the anti-democratic forces in the United States were to succeed in promoting "some kind of fascism" that would encourage "suppressing the bill of rights," "nationalistic jingoism," and "military adventures" abroad,[33] it could do so only through a *disguised* or *dishonest* appeal to the nation's democratic tradition (my italics). Thus, for Counts, the possible ascendance of an authoritarian or fascist political culture in the United States would first require a critical mass of citizens who had *lost* the capacity for distinguishing between true and false representations of democracy. In applying this Countsian lesson to contemporary circumstances, readers would be justified in interpreting Donald Trump's political *modus operandi* of sowing division and doubt as representing exactly the kind of fascist emergence that Counts warned against.

In a sense, readers of *A Call* are compelled to ask the same difficult questions that Jefferson wrestled with centuries before: Were citizens to ever lose their ability to identify disguised appeals to American democracy when they see them, and were they to lose the capacity to distinguish genuine democracy from its ideological counterfeits—then, what would happen to the principle of public intelligence upon which the moral legitimacy of democracy rests? As one way out of what Counts calls the "moral confusion" the country found itself in because of the Great Depression, he urges teachers to reset their vocational identities in very fundamental ways. Teachers could begin

---

[32] *A Call*, 16–17.
[33] Ibid., 17.

this vocational reset by seizing opportunities to exercise "cultural leadership" on behalf of the democratic-revolutionary tradition, both inside and outside the schools.[34]

As Counts articulates his unapologetically biased educational program, we cannot help but be reminded of the curricular features of Jefferson's politically biased educational program. For example, in Chapters 2 and 3, we saw how Jefferson advocated for education's chief civic purpose to be the promotion of the general welfare; moreover, Jefferson proposed that educators and citizens needed to develop a greater knowledge of the aristocratic and monarchical forces and mechanisms that, in his view, would *continuously* pose a threat to America's democratic experiment.

Let's recall that the political knowledge Jefferson wanted to develop within citizens could not accurately be regarded as "politically neutral." In its general orientation, Jefferson's educational program could more accurately be described as simultaneously pro-democratic and anti-aristocratic. It is anti-aristocratic in that Jefferson wants citizens to develop a kind of political knowledge about the power relations and social mechanisms by which elites in past societies operated to usurp the intelligence, engagement, and potential of the people. It was axiomatic that only when a critical mass of the people as a whole were equipped with this form of political knowledge, could such anti-democratic tendencies be effectively checked. And Jefferson's educational program can be regarded as pro-democratic in that it places its faith in the educability of the people as the foundation of its general orientation.

Counts's vision for reconstructing the purposes of public education so that the schools would serve publically defined purposes—rather than corporately defined purposes—can be understood as a twentieth-century reinterpretation of Jefferson's original educational blueprint. Counts argues that while the moral foundations of Jefferson's education have only been partially fulfilled at best, the progressive extension of these values and commitments into the dynamic present would require educational efforts to conserve the memory of the nation's revolutionary democratic tradition.

> Our philosophy of education should be securely rooted in the democratic-revolutionary tradition of the American people, but should bathe its

---

[34] In the context of the early 1930s, we must bear in mind that the teacher union movement, one vital form of cultural leadership, was in its early stages of development.

branches in the atmosphere of industrial civilization and the world of nations.[35]

Counts further unpacks the practical meaning of its curricular aims:

> It should aim to foster in boys and girls a profound sense of human worth, a genuine devotion to the welfare of the masses, a deep aversion to the tyranny of privilege, a warm feeling of kinship with all the races of mankind, and a quick readiness to engage in bold social experimentation.[36]

While Counts does not explicitly discuss the concept of *demophilia*, what he does describe as an underlying educational vision and purpose, would certainly seem to embody an implicit *demophilia*. If Jefferson were somehow to appraise the American cultural scene in the 1920s and 1930s, he would undoubtedly support Count's and Dewey's allied campaigns to re-energize American democracy by seeking to re-energize the democratic purposes of public education. And Jefferson would most assuredly affirm the need to employ education as a means for developing within the young, "a quick readiness to engage in bold social experimentation." Jefferson would recognize, in particular, that without the schools doing what they could to promote in students a participatory readiness to engage in bold social experimentation, we would risk the vestal flame of the republic flickering out.

---

[35] *A Call*, 20–21.

[36] Ibid., 21.

PART II

Declension: Betrayal of Founding Principles

Overview

There are at least three moral and political principles we could identify which gave newly minted Americans a sense of their own exceptionality. The three foundational principles I bracket to illustrate this point are expressed by Jefferson where he argues for the adaption of additional constitutional amendments to the proposed US Constitution. For our present purposes, let's focus specifically on the constitutional amendments Jefferson proposed that did *not* ultimately become codified in the Bill of Rights. To briefly review: Jefferson argued (i) for a prohibition of standing armies; (ii) freedom from corporate monopolies; and (iii) he proposed that a federal education amendment be adopted for a public establishment of education. These proposals, particularly when considered together as a conceptual whole, are worth recalling because they represent some of the most defining yet largely overlooked dimensions of Jefferson's revolutionary theory.

Without too much difficulty, we could identify three corresponding moral and political principles that stand behind and inform each of these constitutional renovations:

(i) That the military power must be limited and made subordinate to the civil power to avoid the development of a permanent war society;

(ii) That corporate power must be limited and made subordinate to the state power, to avoid the inequalities and corruption that accompany corporate monopolies of wealth and power;

(iii) That the federal government should empower an establishment of public education for the purpose of developing an intelligent and alert citizenry.

Although we could identify other foundational principles that helped form the mythological terrain of American exceptionalism during the early republic, the amendments that Jefferson championed and the principles and values they symbolize are crucial because they are conceptually inseparable from Jefferson's revolutionary thought. As we've seen, for Jefferson, the political, the economic, and the educational domains were all interconnected. Generally stated, we could say that, for Jefferson, revolutionary processes would grind to a halt in the United States were it to become a permanent war society; were it to become dominated by corporate power; and were its citizens to become unintelligent, distracted, and easily manipulated by ambitious would-be tyrants. In other words, Jefferson's proposed amendments were intended to protect against specific political, economic, and educational threats that he thought were most likely to deteriorate America's fragile experiment in self-government.

When we consider the moral and democratic ideals underlying these amendments in light of the defining structural features of our own historical moment, we cannot help but recognize at least three emerging trends. The United States has indeed become a permanent warfare state; it has indeed become increasingly corporate-dominated and rent with class inequality and corruption; and recently, the purposes of public education clearly seem far more oligarchic than democratic in character. Of course, the triad of Jeffersonian moral principles underlying these proposed amendments still exist today, even if un-enacted in a formal constitutional sense. This betrayal and subsequent cultural amnesia forms the basis of a kind of jeremiadic declension, a moral and political devolution that has caused an intensification of contradictions between the ideal and the reality of America's mythological self-conception. As is implied throughout Part II, it should be regarded as a healthy exercise to try and recover the memory and tradition of these amendments. Engaging in such a thought experiment can hopefully serve both as a critique of the present and as a stimulus to excite our democratic moral imaginations.

Jefferson frequently referred to Europe's ruling monarchical regimes with barely concealed contempt. While Jefferson certainly valued and admired Europe's cultural and scientific achievements, he also made clear that the culture and government of the United States had to define and organize itself in radical opposition to core monarchical institutions, such as standing armies, corporate monopolies, and to the official policy of encouraging illiteracy and ignorance among the mass of people. In crucial respects, then, each of the three amendments envisioned by Jefferson represents not only core theoretical components of his revolutionary theory but, in a related sense, three strands of American exceptionalism itself. As discussed in previous chapters, Jefferson's theory is holistic: for it to hang together conceptually, the right kind of republican institutions had to be furnished in order to provide the right kind of political, economic, and educational conditions for keeping constant the movement toward democratization.

Practically speaking, Jefferson's theory holds that, were Americans to lose sight of their revolutionary origins and try merely to emulate Europe, or to not take care to uproot certain ideological inheritances, the nation's capacity to morally renovate its experiment in self-government would be fatally doomed.

CHAPTER 6

To Protect Against Standing Armies

Historical Context

When Jefferson gazed across the Atlantic and referred to the "exterminating havoc" of Europe, he was describing in large part the deadly and oppressive consequences of maintaining standing armies as institutions in perpetuity.[1] Jefferson's disenchantment with British standing armies in colonial America had been longstanding. While serving as minister to France after independence, he had also witnessed firsthand the myriad ways in which standing armies helped to fortify and uphold aristocratic monarchies across Europe.

In Jefferson's mind, as noted in previous chapters, the success of the American Revolution depended on several institutional anchors, and foremost among them was the legal and political subordination of the military to the civil power. Writing to James Madison in 1787, Jefferson argued that the new Constitution that was being hammered out in Philadelphia should include an amendment stipulating "protection against standing armies."[2] The purpose of Jefferson's amendment was to make this legal and political subordination one of the explicit moral cornerstones of

---

[1] Thomas Jefferson, First Inaugural Address, March 4, 1801. In Merrill D. Peterson, ed., *Thomas Jefferson: Writings.* Washington, DC: The Library of America, 1984, 492–496. Unless otherwise indicated, all of Jefferson's citations are from this text.

[2] Thomas Jefferson to James Madison, December 20, 1787, 916.

© The Author(s) 2020
K. T. Burch, *Jefferson's Revolutionary Theory and the Reconstruction of Educational Purpose,* The Cultural and Social Foundations of Education, https://doi.org/10.1007/978-3-030-45763-1_6

America's exceptional identity. Unlike the war-drenched European states, the United States would organize itself on a peaceful basis, without resort to standing armies. For the American Revolution to become continuous, as Jefferson theorized, an enduring institutional basis for permanent peace needed to be codified as a specifically enumerated right. Placed in a broader constitutional context, for example, the people's inalienable right to the pursuit of happiness, could not be fully protected unless it also included their right to be free from the institutionalization of war—and significantly, free from the problematic domestic consequences that Jefferson and others believed would always accompany the presence of standing armies.

As we know, no such amendment was included within the Bill of Rights. Yet, the influence of the proposal's moral spirit in the public imagination still had to be reckoned with. Its cultural force, as a form of common sense, could be seen to have shaped key aspects of the Constitution's design, albeit in diluted form. For instance, Article 1 Section 8 places the war-making power with Congress rather than with the Executive, in an attempt to democratize the crucial war-making power. Similarly, a limitation was placed on military establishments, so that any appropriation made by Congress to the military could not exceed two years in duration. In another indirect form of constitutional protection against standing armies, the Second Amendment's guarantee to the state's that they could form local militias was intended, at least according to some interpretations, precisely to circumvent the need for the federal government to create a permanent standing army.[3]

The Declaration, for its part, directs several rhetorical salvos against standing armies. In the list of grievances section, Jefferson establishes that: "He has kept among us in times of peace, standing armies without the consent of the legislature." Jefferson continues however to link the existence of standing armies to a set of other problems, such as mock trials of soldiers accused of abusing civilians, the quartering of soldiers in personal residences, and the dread "writs of assistance," arbitrary legal

---

[3] See, for example, Carl T. Bogus, ed., *The Second Amendment in Law and History: Historians and Constitutional Scholars on the Right to Bear Arms*. New York: The New Press, 2002; Thom Hartmann, *The Hidden History of Guns and the Second Amendment*. San Francisco: Berrett-Koehler, 2019.

instruments which authorized warrantless searches and seizures.[4] For the purposes of this chapter, it's crucial for readers to hold these domestic, non-lethal oppressions in mind, as they were so closely tied to standing armies within the emerging American mind.

The Declaration further charges that England's military power in the colonies was constructed as something beyond the reach of any countervailing civil power. "He has," Jefferson writes, "affected to render the military independent of and superior to the civil power." Jefferson's enlightenment conception of the Idea of America moved him to insist that the civil power must be constructed as independent of, and superior to, any military power. In theory, by erecting constitutional barriers to protect against standing armies, Jefferson wanted to link the foundational premises of America's exceptional character to this enlightenment-inspired moral renovation. Again, along with others of the revolutionary generation, he assumed that the perpetuation of standing armies would eventually mean not only that the military power would be elevated to a position independent of, and superior to, the civil power, but that this structuring of power would virtually guarantee the formation of a permanent war society. Such an eventuality would at once roll-back crucial Enlightenment gains and demolish the claim of America's presumed exceptionality.

Americans also need to appreciate today that the critical spirit animating anti-standing army ideology was "baked into" many state constitutions. This suggests that the critical spirit animating anti-war ideology had achieved a critical mass of popular support. As Arthur A. Ekirch's classic study of the anti-militarist tradition in the United States demonstrates, many state constitutions, before and after 1776, contained provisions prohibiting standing armies.[5] Americans of the revolutionary generation developed a keen awareness of how this European institution stood in direct contradiction to the values, purposes, and identity of America's republican experiment. More recently, Andrew Bacevich underscored the existence of this once dominant historical consciousness: "The Founders, the commander of the Continental Army not least among them, disparaged standing armies as inconsistent with republican virtue while posing a

---

[4] See, for example, Chris Hedges, "The Post-Constitutional Era." In *Wages of Rebellion: The Moral Imperative of Revolt.* New York: Nation Books, 2015, 55.

[5] Arthur A. Ekirch, Jr., *The Civilian and the Military.* New York: Oxford University Press, 1956.

visceral threat to republican institutions."[6] It is warranted, then, to interpret the strong aversion to standing armies in the early republic to reflect a widely held form of common sense. It was the content and quality of this common sense that was foundational in both igniting the American Revolution and in shaping subsequent debates about how the civil/military division of power within the Constitution would be legally and politically structured.

JEFFERSON'S PROPOSAL AND EISENHOWER'S MILITARY–INDUSTRIAL COMPLEX

Our discussion of the larger historical context of Jefferson's principled opposition to standing armies would be incomplete without reference to President Dwight D. Eisenhower's farewell address (1961). Eisenhower's nationally televised speech introduced the term "military-industrial complex" into the nation's lexicon. Many commentators have mapped the ever-expanding, now ubiquitous scope of this system of power. It is a tricky system of power for us to conceptualize. In part, this is because it's a system which can be interpreted both as an empirically verifiable institutional construct, as well as a deeply gendered social imaginary.[7] For our purposes, however, Eisenhower's farewell can be situated as a kind of executive jeremiad on the dangers posed to the nation's democratic spirit by the military–industrial complex. As I make the case in the following passages, it should be no huge leap to recognize that today's military–industrial complex can be seen to represent the moral and political equivalent of a inordinantly powerful standing army—even as we recognize that today's version eclipses in scope the traditional boundaries of the concept.

At the moral core of Eisenhower's speech is the admonition that Americans needed to think anew about the existential threat posed to the nation's democratic heritage by the militarization of its identity. Although

---

[6] Andrew Bacevich, *Washington Rules: America's Path to Permanent War*. New York: Metropolitan Books, 2010, 243–244.

[7] For an excellent contemporary interpretation of the military–industrial complex, see James Ledbetter, *Unwarranted Influence: Dwight D. Eisenhower and the Military-Industrial Complex*. New Haven, CT: Yale University Press, 2010. For a gendered and psychological interpretation of "the complex," see Kerry Burch, "Rereading the "Complex" Psychologically: Toward a Theory of America's Civic Neurosis." In *Democratic Transformations: Eight Conflicts in the Negotiation of American Identity*. New York: Bloomsbury, 2012, 126–133.

Eisenhower never explicitly mentions the institution of standing armies per se, he certainly does so implicitly, in a manner consistent with mid-twentieth-century conditions. In effect, Ike told the nation that the growing power of the military–industrial complex was producing the same set of antidemocratic domestic consequences that traditional standing armies were typically known to produce. A critical examination of Ike's text, particularly when read in light of Jefferson's proposed amendment, suggests that, underneath these two signifiers, *standing army* and *military–industrial complex*, sits the same existential danger. Namely, that of the military power achieving supremacy over the civil power. Eisenhower defines the depth of the problem:

> We have been compelled to create a permanent armaments industry of vast proportions. We annually spend on military security alone more than the net income of all United States corporations. The conjunction of an immense military establishment and a large arms industry is new in the American experience." The total influence—economic, political, *even spiritual*—is felt in every city, every statehouse, every office of federal government.[8]

It is significant, I think, that Eisenhower sees fit to add the words, *even spiritual*, when describing the "total influence" that the military–industrial complex was exercising on the moral integrity of the national identity. When Ike refers to the corrosive spiritual effects of militarism on America's democratic heritage, he expresses the historically rooted fear that militarism's values, perceptions, and habits of mind could all too easily become normalized within the popular imagination. As if to underscore the danger posed to the nation's identity by the over-valorization of military values and modes of perception, Eisenhower held a press conference the day following his farewell in which he reiterated that an "inordinate preoccupation with military solutions" would produce "an insidious penetration of our own minds."[9] Here, Eisenhower seems to be echoing Jefferson: He wanted the military to protect the nation—not to define it.

For all of these reasons, then, we can interpret Eisenhower's dire warning as an historical extension of Jefferson's earlier critique of standing

---

[8] Dwight D. Eisenhower, Farewell Address, January 17, 1961. As quoted in Ledbetter, 211–220.

[9] Ledbetter, 96.

armies. It appears that Jefferson and Eisenhower, each employing their own idioms and writing from their own historical locations, were attempting to heighten public awareness about what they saw as a fatal symbiosis between the militarization of American identity, on the one hand, and a corresponding loss of its democratic soul on the other.

To unpack this purported causal relation between the militarization of American identity and the corresponding loss of its democratic soul, we might examine how this same insight and interpretation emerged as a central organizing principle of Martin Luther King's framework for criticizing American society, particularly during the 1967–68 period. As other noted thinkers have articulated, King came to see that the indicia of social misery in the US (caused by militarism, poverty, and racism) could not be remedied so long as they were understood in conceptual isolation.[10] King was emphatic that only in "knowing" how these problems formed a conceptual whole, could the American people meaningfully address and ameliorate these structural oppressions. Couched in contemporary terms, it's fair to say that King sought to understand these problems on the basis of their *intersectionality* (an expression he never used, but would have appreciated). To resist and counteract these overlapping structural oppressions, King's later jeremiads held that the country's redemption could only be meaningfully achieved by redirecting our massive expenditures on war to that of expenditures on broad-based programs of social uplift. Interestingly enough, Jefferson, in justifying his federal education amendment to the Constitution, similarly warned how, in the absence of constitutional protection, expenditures for war would always stand in the way of expenditures for establishing public education (see Chapter 8).

King was inexorably led to the realization that the logic and values of the military had, as Jefferson and Eisenhower had foreseen, produced an "insidious penetration of [the American] mind." The cultural implantation of militarism into the nation's soul-life was poignantly if tragically captured when King soberly observed: "A nation that continues year after year to spend more money on military defense than on

---

[10] Two valuable sources on King's critique of American militarism, in addition to MLKs own writings, can be found in Cornel West, *The Radical King*. Boston: Beacon Press, 2015, and more recently, eds. Tommie Shelby and Brandon Terry, *To Shape a New World: Essays on the Political Philosophy of Martin Luther King, Jr*. Cambridge: Harvard University Press, 2018.

programs of social uplift is approaching spiritual death."[11] It is indeed sobering to reflect that, in the five decades since King spoke these words, the ratio of military spending relative to spending on programs of social uplift has widened to a breathtaking degree.[12] Considering the vast cultural power that military values and authority command in American society today, no serious observer could deny that the worst fears of Jefferson, Eisenhower, and King have been fully realized.

Yet, even as we recognize the undeniable historical trend toward the institutionalization of military supremacy in American life, it would be idle to suggest that these deeply entrenched structures can be easily transformed, much less "abolished." The military–industrial complex of today, as has been suggested, represents a massive extension of the eighteenth-century version of a standing army. While we may not be able to reverse the inordinate militarization of American society and identity as quickly or as easily as we would like, anti-militarist civic educators can still attempt to retrieve the moral spirit that informs Jefferson's constitutional proposal. Thus, in the following section, I hope to identify the essential features of that moral spirit through an interpretation of a contemporary moral controversy, one that is deeply implicated in the militarization of American cultural identity.

EDWARD SNOWDEN AS A GOOD REBEL: A JEFFERSONIAN DEFENSE

How, then, to recover the moral spirit of Jefferson's proposed constitutional amendment to "protect against standing armies"? How might such a recovery be integrated into our pedagogical practice? I want to engage this thought experiment in the context of the Edward Snowden controversy. Given Jefferson's rejection of the so-called reason of state ideology, his moral sense philosophy, and his broader revolutionary theory, we have more than a sufficient basis from which to interpret the Snowden controversy through a Jeffersonian conceptual prism.

---

[11] Martin Luther King, Jr. "Beyond Vietnam: A Time to Break Silence," April 4, 1967. As quoted in Cornel West's *The Radical King*, 215 (see Footnote 10).

[12] An excellent source of information is Brown University's Costs of War Project, Watson Institute, International & Public Affairs, Brown University. https://watson.brown.edu/costsofwar.

It is well known that Snowden deliberately violated certain secrecy laws of the US government, fled the country to elude capture, and is currently living in exile in Russia.[13] In a strictly legal sense, Snowden's "crime" of releasing highly classified material to the public is not under dispute. What is under dispute, however, is how to interpret the moral dimensions of Snowden's action, particularly in light of Jefferson's respect for the role of dissent in a democratic republic. Ultimately, Snowden's act of resistance is morally ambiguous because his motivation for releasing the classified material was to inform the public that its government was massively engaging in witting unconstitutional conduct, in real time. According to Snowden, the unprecedented scale of surveillance that he discovered constituted a crime against the American people (represented principally by the Constitution and its Fourth and Fifth Amendments).[14] The release and publication of the Snowden files in 2013 provide compelling empirical evidence that the electronic communications of all Americans were being "swept up" without their knowledge by sophisticated surveillance technologies operating under the authority of the National Security Agency. What makes Snowden's alleged crime even more complex is that it has created a substantially more honest political environment in which Americans can debate the legitimacy and scope of the state's surveillance powers.

Snowden's detractors in the United States rely for the most part on conventional "reason of state" arguments to support their positions. The reason of state theory occupies a long-standing place within the western political tradition.[15] As a discourse it has generally been deployed to justify a "might makes right" political ideology, an ideology whose framework assumes that an act may be undertaken by a state provided that such action is seen to preserve the state's power and existence. On this point, it is significant that Jefferson, as a constitutional lawyer himself, understood

[13] Snowden's recently published memoir provides much, but not all of the material for my analysis. See, Edward Snowden, *Permanent Record*. New York: Metropolitan Books, 2019.

[14] Ibid., 1–8.

[15] Although the literature on this theory is vast, this section of the chapter relies on two sources. Nancy L. Rosenblum's "Constitutional Reason of State: The Fear Factor." In *Dissent in Dangerous Times*, ed. Austin Sarat. Ann Arbor: The University of Michigan Press, 2008, 146–175. For Jefferson's rejection of established reason of state arguments, I rely on Robert W. Tucker and David C. Hendrickson, *Empire of Liberty: The Statecraft of Thomas Jefferson*. New York, NY: Oxford University Press, 1990.

the history of the reason of state argument and rejected it as unbecoming of the new American state.[16]

Writing in the *New Yorker* legal analyst Jeffrey Toobin's article, "Edward Snowden is No Hero," sums up Snowden as a "grandiose narcissist who deserves to be in prison."[17] Working comfortably within a reason of state perspective, Toobin asks in so many words: Who is this Snowden character to defy the self-evident wisdom of state power? Writing in juxtaposition to Toobin in the same issue of the *New Yorker*, John Cassidy, in his piece, "Why Edward Snowden Is a Hero," makes the case that Snowden's decision to expose the state's role in unconstitutional conduct was the morally correct and courageous thing to do."[18] Cassidy thus interprets the controversy from a less state-centric, more Jeffersonian perspective.

Let us proceed, then, on the premise that one of the conflicts at the core of the controversy—Snowden's identity as a good rebel, or as someone who committed treason against the United States—presents us with a potentially educative contradiction. The contradiction could be identified and developed in many ways, but for our purposes, let's bracket the nucleus of the conflict as a conflict between the moral principles identified within the Declaration of Independence and the preamble to the US Constitution, on the one hand, and the body of the Constitution, including its binding legislation and judicial rulings, on the other. A cursory review of American history demonstrates that the laws governing the Constitution have not always been in alignment with the moral principles enshrined in the Declaration and preamble. The productive tensions generated from this conflict between the nation's birth certificates should be more broadly understood than it is today, as that which propels the trajectory of American political history and gives shape to its ongoing public debates. In transforming the Snowden controversy into a site of critical analysis within our classrooms, we can create opportunities to make education out of the contradictory nucleus of American political culture.

To better grasp the linkages that connect the prohibition of standing armies to the moral and political issues at stake in the Snowden controversy, we need first to recall that the Declaration named several ways in

[16] See above, *Empire of Liberty*, 10–17.
[17] Jeffrey Toobin, "Edward Snowden Is No Hero." *New Yorker*, June 10, 1013.
[18] John Cassidy, "Why Edward Snowden Is a Hero." *New Yorker*, June 10, 2013.

which standing armies could abuse their powers. Their potential for the abuse of power extended beyond waging perpetual war. The power of standing armies could also be abused in times of peace whenever they served the broader purposes of political repression. The *absolute power* that standing armies could potentially manifest was what enabled the writs of assistance and other abuses which so infuriated revolutionary-era Americans. To reiterate, then, emerging from the revolutionary period was a commonsense conviction that when *any* institution, military, corporate, or state-oriented, wielded *any* form of absolute power, tyranny, and corruption were sure to follow.

According to his own account, Snowden began to see that the unchecked surveillance powers of the US government had become effectively militarized:

> When armies are shooting at each other, there's no room for a judge on that battlefield. But now the government had decided—without the public's participation, without our knowledge and consent—that the battlefield is everywhere. Individuals who don't represent an imminent threat in any meaningful sense of those words are redefined, through the subversion of language, to meet that definition.[19]

Snowden's contention that the "battlefield is everywhere" tacitly recognizes that the traditional boundaries of military authority and power are far too limited to capture the ubiquitous, "full-spectrum dominance" of America's military power today. And even if we fully appreciate the chasm in historical time that separates the eighteenth from the twenty-first centuries, it shouldn't be too difficult for us to recognize the ideological similitude between the absolute power that Jefferson intended to protect against in relation to standing armies, and the absolute power that Snowden intended to protect against in relation to the militarization of the intelligence security establishment.

No doubt, the present-day institutional structure of the National Security State is far more capacious, physically, than the eighteenth-century model of a standing army. However, despite this variation of physical or institutional breadth, when these two historical formations are examined

[19] Edward Snowden, "Inside the Assassination Complex: Whistleblowing Is Not Just Leaking—It's an Act of Political Resistance." *The Intercept.* https://theintercept.com/2016/05/03/edward-snowwden-whistleblowing-is-not-just-leaking, 12.

from an ideological or cultural standpoint, that is, from the standpoint of the moral and political purposes they embody, striking parallels emerge. Each historical formation, for example, manifests a form of absolute power and each tends to advance elite-aristocratic purposes, political characteristics, and aims that must be viewed as threats to any viable notion of republican self-government. It is notoriously difficult for critical commentators to theorize the fluid and expansive boundaries of what we're calling the military–industrial complex. Among other difficulties, today's military–industrial complex is so ubiquitous it's hard to wrap one's conceptual arms around the whole thing. Perhaps what critics of militarism struggle to name today could be described as a *globalized cyber-verse model* of a standing army, where the "battlefield is everywhere," forming a vast network of unaccountable, disciplinary power that amplifies a thousand-fold the potentially abusive powers of the eighteenth-century model of the standing army.[20]

REFLECTIONS ON THE EDUCATION OF SNOWDEN'S MORAL SENSE

One of the most instructive features of Snowden's case is the manner in which he articulates the moral justification for his decision to resist and act. Snowden, it must be noted, has never ascribed any heroic intentions or attributes to his whistleblowing, but rather emphasizes that he was acting in his capacity as a citizen. By the time Snowden reached twenty-nine years old, he had already managed to jettison himself into the upper echelons of the national security establishment. Owing to nothing but his incredible computer acumen, Snowden attained a rarified level of access to highly classified information. For someone who was enormously bored by school and dropped out at the age of fifteen, and with no credentials in higher education, Snowden's trajectory qualifies as remarkable.

Snowden tells us that what he learned while working with the CIA, and with the private intelligence contractor, Booz Allen and Hamilton, increasingly disturbed his conscience. In Jeffersonian terms, Snowden experienced a disturbance within his moral sense. As we've already discussed, in a uniquely American context, this intuitive capacity finds much of its anchorage in the mythopoetic field of meaning Jefferson called

---

[20] Tom Engelhardt, *A Nation Unmade by War*. Chicago: Haymarket Books, 2018.

the Spirit of 76. The motivation for Snowden's resistance appears to be traced to the power of this mythical terrain, where democratic moral precepts like equality, individual liberty, and freedom—including restraint on unchecked power—constitute a thematic field of meaning.[21] The prior existence of this meaning narrative within Snowden, as a set of internalized moral and civic values, was poised to collide with the oncoming train of his new and dangerous knowledge. This interior moral collision sharpened Snowden's commitment to the principles of the Constitution over and above the reason of state principle that, much to his dismay, dominated the highest echelons of the national security establishment.

Snowden's account of the changes in his thinking in the months leading up to his fateful action, reflects the psychic disequilibrium that he experienced as a consequence of acquiring a new and potentially dangerous knowledge. The psychic disturbances it caused gave rise to an agonizing moral predicament.

> I realized that they were building a system whose goal was the elimination of all privacy, globally. To make it so that no one could communicate electronically without the NSA being able to collect, store, and analyze the communication...I do not want to live in a world where we have no privacy and no freedom, where the unique values of the Internet is snuffed out.[22]

Here, and throughout his public statements and writings, Snowden expresses a high degree of receptivity to, and identification with, the nation's constitutional tradition. In discussing what he takes to be the deeper meanings of the Constitution and the genius that informed it, Snowden observes: Our founding impulse was to say, "*Though we are mighty, we are voluntarily restrained.*"[23] With this assertion, Snowden does a fantastic job of articulating one of the principles that was supposed to define American exceptionalism—the idea that a state's potential power to destroy must be willingly restrained. We could surmise that Snowden's moral sense, self-consciously rooted in the best of the American political

---

[21] See, for example, the chapter "Whistleblowing," in his *Permanent Record*, 227–235.

[22] This passage comes from an interview of Snowden by Glenn Greenwald. See, Glenn Greenwald, *No Place to Hide: Edward Snowden, the NSA and the US Surveillance State*. New York: Henry Holt, 2014, 47–48.

[23] As quoted in *The Intercept*, 11, see Footnote 19.

tradition, revolted against the knowledge that the constitutional principles he loved were being secretly violated without the consent of the American people.

Maintaining the integrity of the negative freedoms guaranteed within the Fourth Amendment (protection against warrantless searches and seizures) is the immediate reason why Snowden performed this act of civil disobedience. For Snowden, the motive for undertaking this formally illegal civic action was to protect the republic from itself by bestowing the power of knowledge and truth to the American people. In this way, Snowden could be understood as a Socratic figure—someone who committed the "crime" of forcing the state to examine its morally bankrupt conduct.

Snowden expects that the constitutional restraints must also protect the public sphere function of the Internet. The integrity of the Internet, he argues, must be maintained above all because it's the space in which personal knowledge quests can take place. "For many kids, the Internet is a means of self-actualization," Snowden tells Greenwald. "It allows them to explore who they are and who they want to be, but that works only if we're able to be private and anonymous, to make mistakes without them following us. I worry that mine was the last generation to enjoy that freedom"[24]

Snowden walks readers through his moral reasoning:

> And when you're confronted with evidence—not in an edge case, not in a peculiarity, but as a core consequence of the program—that the government is subverting the Constitution and violating the ideals you so fervently believe in, you have to make a decision. When you see that the program or policy is inconsistent with the oaths and obligations that you've sworn to your society and yourself, then that oath and that obligation cannot be reconciled with the program. To which do you owe a greater allegiance?[25]

In the Greenwald interview, Snowden says he reached the point where his stated beliefs and the identity he constructed for himself would mean nothing if he wasn't willing to act—and risk his own life—on behalf of those beliefs and values. "The true measurement of a person's worth isn't what they say they believe in, but what they do in defense of those beliefs.

[24] Greenwald, 46.
[25] Snowden, *The Intercept*, 9.

If you're not acting on your beliefs, then they probably aren't real."[26] Whatever one may think about Snowden's ethical decision-making, he certainly furnishes an articulate moral justification for what he calls his "political resistance." The biggest lesson here is that Snowden exhibits an unusually strong identification with, and emotional attachment to, a kind of republican-indebted moral sense, an intuitive capacity which, as we've seen, Jefferson theorized as the imaginative seedbed from which could spring successive renovations of the American revolution.

A Jeffersonian interpretation of Snowden's education and character formation would have to take serious note of Snowden's highly developed moral sense. Such an interpretation would also suggest that, however paradoxical it may seem, Snowden's absence of exposure to formal higher education may have constituted a sound basis for the positive development of his moral sense. Because the development of the moral sense does not owe its existence to formal education, the relative absence of formal or higher education in Snowden's life may have prevented him from being "led astray" by its potentially dulling and obedience-laden rules. The logic of this analysis forces upon us the following question: Did Snowden's non-experience in higher education provide him with the necessary open spaces within which his moral decision-making capacities could develop to the extraordinary degree that they did?

It's worth recalling in Chapter 3 that Jefferson's moral sense philosophy is crystallized through his "ploughman and professor" allegory. "State a moral case to a ploughman and a professor," Jefferson declares, "and the former will decide it as well, and often better than the latter, because he has *not been led astray by artificial rules.*"[27] According to Jefferson, development of the moral sense bore little if any relation to formal education as such—emphasis on canonical disputes and abstract rules within the field of moral philosophy could only distract one from developing a felt, visceral relation to this intuitive human capacity. A Jeffersonian interpretation of Snowden's education might further suggest that Snowden actually experienced a stellar, world-class education—but it had a heterodox quality, occurring outside the boundaries of formal schooling. The Internet gave to Snowden a boundary-less, world-class education, but in

---

[26] Greenwald, 45.

[27] Thomas Jefferson to Peter Carr, August 10, 1787.

any case, an education that included a deeply felt understanding of the highest ideals of the nation's political tradition.

The Snowden controversy invites us to consider: What kind of citizens do we want to create? Certainly, we don't want to form citizens who are conditioned *not to see* constitutional violations or, when seen, to see them without hint of indignation. It seems to me that a citizen like Snowden could serve as a useful prototype for intelligent and committed citizenship. Snowden could model a good, rebellious form of citizenship owing to his knowledge of, and fidelity to, the moral and political principles of the Declaration and Constitution, a civic orientation that would take precedence over fidelity to those who hold offices of state at any given time. Is it not ironic, then, that Snowden's ardent love of the nation's politcal tradition is what caused his legal trouble?

We shall never know how Jefferson might have advised Snowden as he wrestled with these ethical dilemmas. However, given Jefferson's strong opposition to the absolute power of standing armies, given his rejection of reason of state ideology, and given his enlightenment-oriented moral sense philosophy, we have a reasonable basis for thinking that the sage of Monticello would have been among the first of the founders to come to Snowden's defense.

LESSONS FROM THE SNOWDEN CASE: OR, HOW TO MAKE THE LOVE OF DEMOCRACY INTUITIVE?

This fleeting excursion into the Snowden controversy cannot hope to treat the subject as thoroughly as it deserves. Many important dimensions of the case have been left unaddressed, many questions unasked; yet, considering the chapter's limited aims, a partial treatment of the controversy was unavoidable. To conclude the chapter, I state in capsule form some of the educational implications of the Snowden controversy, while also suggesting how these implications can be situated alongside both Jefferson's constitutional proposal and his revolutionary theory.

Edward Snowden can model for our students what it means to be a good rebel and citizen simultaneously. First, let us recall in previous chapters that Danielle Allen's moral ideal of "participatory readiness" was cited as a gold standard for defining the ultimate aim of democratic citizenship. The crucial ethical component of participatory readiness was seen to have captured exactly the model of citizenship that Jefferson had envisioned. It was also noted that the human capacity to revise, constituted the ontological, or experiential, basis of participatory readiness (as a state of heart & mind).

Snowden's practices of citizenship embody several elements that reflect the moral ideal of participatory readiness. Among other things, he exemplifies a capacity to revise oneself, to judge and to choose, to be willing to act, and to fight for a moral ideal. These general traits are implicit within the moral ideal of participatory readiness. On a Jeffersonian basis, then, we could frame the psychic and civic state of participatory readiness as that which is required for the creative enactment of intelligent dissent.

Snowden personifies a synthesis of rebellion and citizenship in a second Jeffersonian sense: his highly developed historical awareness of, and visceral felt relation to, the nation's political and constitutional tradition, were the motivating factors in his willingness to protect that tradition at the risk of his own life and freedom. As was discussed in previous chapters, Jefferson wanted the public schools to cultivate a kind of political knowledge among students—not merely rote knowledge of historical facts. Through a knowledge of the lessons of history he wanted to familiarize the young with the moral vulnerabilities and social mechanisms by which republics have fallen and tyrannies have risen. Snowden came to understand these American constitutional principles not just intellectually but morally, that is, he "knew" these civic symbols and ideals at a gut level. In understanding them at a gut level, he would therefore become indignant when witnessing the violation of something he loved. Snowden, in the language of Jefferson, was "enabled to know ambition under all its shapes," and was "prompt to exert his natural powers to defeat its purposes." An examination of the Snowden case shows us that the development of a felt, visceral relation to the nation's democratic and constitutional heritage, just as Jefferson had hoped, would form persons willing to engage in acts of political creativity. Citizens like Snowden, in other words, can spark revolutionary processes of transition, precisely because they love the nation's constitutional tradition.

The third sense in which Snowden stands as a model of good rebellious citizenship, concerns his effort to enlighten a previously unenlightened public. Snowden's mission to bring the light of knowledge and truth to the American public was motivated by a desire to create the conditions in which an authentic, truth-based debate about the state's escalating surveillance powers could occur in the public sphere. Snowden thus symbolizes a kind of citizen who trusts in the intelligence of ordinary people to act reasonably, provided, of course, they are properly informed. He cares about their welfare and, similar to Jefferson, seems to believe that the integrity of the democratic experiment depends on cultivating the public's general intelligence, particularly as that intelligence relates to perceiving constitutional violations. Snowden's politically creative resistance on behalf of the people—rather than being identified as a *crime* by the US government could with ample justification be identified as a form of *demophilia*.

It is commonplace to note that bringing the light of knowledge and a broader civic awareness to human beings who were previously without such knowledge and awareness, has always proven to be a dangerous, tragic enterprise. Dangerous to the established order and frequently tragic to the bringers of light. To illustrate how this foundational educational motif works in relation to the Snowden case, let's recall that before he released reams of classified documents to the public, perhaps several hundred individuals, sworn to secrecy, knew about the *en masse* surveillance being conducted on Americans (and other global inhabitants) by the NSA. After Snowden's disclosures, now hundreds of millions of citizens across the nation (and world) gained new knowledge of the existence of these unconstitutional programs and operations. Snowden has maintained all along that his purpose was to reform and restrain the powers of the military/intelligence establishment, not to destroy them. And Snowden's political resistance has introduced a vital new element into American society that was missing before—a more truthful perception among Americans of "conditions as they are, the only solid basis for communication."[28] Snowden's dissent thus marks a significant contribution to ongoing debates regarding the ethical predicaments of living in an increasingly militarized and surveillant society. How could Jefferson not defend a person who so clearly enhanced the truth environment of American political culture?

[28] This foundational premise of democratic culture is taken from Dewey's, "Creative Democracy—The Task Before Us" (1939). Arguably, this article represents the most cogent interpretation of the meaning of democracy in the nation's democratic canon. It is noted here to underscore its obvious connection to Jefferson's democratic and ethical conception of political knowledge, whereby "knowledge of conditions as they are" is prerequisite for acting intelligently and ethically. For full citation see Chapter 4, Footnote 32.

CHAPTER 7

Freedom from Monopolies

Historical Context

We can begin to grasp the inner meaning of Jefferson's proposal to place a constitutional restriction on monopolies by recalling the 1773 Boston Tea Party. The destruction of the East India Tea Company's inventory, and the core issue it symbolized, has been recognized as one of the root causes of the American Revolution. Simply put, the problem of monopoly power was at the center of the conflict. The "tea action," as its participants called it, was a momentous act of anti-corporate civil disobedience.[1] The tea action helped mobilize public opinion against the tyranny of British power, a form of power that, over time, more and more Americans regarded as inseparable from the enforcement of commercial monopolies.

Jefferson articulated the extent of this problem in his widely read manifesto *A Summary View of the Rights of British America* (1774).[2] It wasn't merely the monopoly power over tea markets that was objectionable

---

[1] See Alfred Young, *The Shoemaker and the Tea Party: Memory and the American Revolution*. Boston: Beacon Press, 1999.

[2] Thomas Jefferson, "A Summary View of the Rights of British America." In *Thomas Jefferson: Writings*, ed. Merrill D. Peterson. New York, NY: Library of America.

© The Author(s) 2020   109
K. T. Burch, *Jefferson's Revolutionary Theory and the Reconstruction of Educational Purpose*, The Cultural and Social Foundations of Education, https://doi.org/10.1007/978-3-030-45763-1_7

and oppressive. A whole edifice of legal monopolies and forms of regulation imposed upon the colonies controlled the manufacture of a range of everyday items, such as hats, paper, and iron. These politico-economic measures transformed the colonies into a structural dependency.[3]

The enthusiastic reception that Jefferson's manifesto received catapulted him onto the national stage and established for many colonial Americans a persuasive set of moral justifications for emancipating themselves psychologically from their "parent" nation.[4] For Jefferson, as we've seen, any dependent power relation by definition would contain germs of corruption. Owing to the fact that monopolies both concentrated economic power and tended invariably to elevate private interests over public interests, their unregulated existence raised grave suspicions in Jefferson's mind. It's a testament to Jefferson's democratic credentials that he foresaw that the corporate form was particularly liable to anti-republican corruption well before the full scope of its power had matured, historically speaking.[5]

To clarify one of the chapter's principle assertions, then, we need to revisit one of the Declaration's most radical claims, namely, the self-evident truth that the government's purpose was to promote "life, liberty and the pursuit of happiness." What we often overlook about this iconic phrase is the sense in which it contains an implicit yet significant demotion of monopoly power and its corrupting influences. The phrases' deeper meaning can be interpreted in this manner if we appreciate that Jefferson, while borrowing part of John Locke's oft-noted formulation of "life, liberty and property," quite deliberately omitted the last term, the protection of property, as one of the defining purposes of the government of the United States. If Pauline Maier's and Danielle Allen's interpretations of the Declaration are correct, that charter's bold move to redefine

---

[3] Ibid., 110–111.

[4] For more on the parental or generational dimensions of the American Revolution, see Catherine L. Albanese, *The Sons of the Fathers: The Civil Religion of the American Revolution*. Philadelphia: Temple University Press, 1977.

[5] The historian Charles Beard offers a Jeffersonian interpretation of the corporate form, at least up to the 1930s. See Charles Beard, *Jefferson, Corporations and the Constitution*. Washington, DC: National Home Library Foundation, 1936.

the purpose of the new government *away* from the protection of property and *toward* the protection of human rights, was not merely Jefferson's personal preference.[6] Significantly, the new enlightenment-inspired definition of the purpose of government reflected the prevailing common sense of the American people—thus, Jefferson and the Continental Congress acted as scribes who were able to capture a snapshot of the emergent American zeitgeist.

In excluding the protection of property as a defining purpose of government—and in promoting a constitutional amendment a decade later to prohibit monopolies—Jefferson was determined to guard against his expectation that corporations would always seek to establish themselves as legal monopolies, as sovereign powers existing outside the reach of popular majorities and governmental "interference." Viewing the arc of the nation's political history from a contemporary perspective, Jefferson's expectation that the elite-aristocratic class would ceaselessly attempt to concentrate economic power through the formation of corporate monopolies, seems prescient as ever.

It bears repeating that for Jefferson and for many of the revolutionary generation, the elevation of human rights over property rights constituted one of the reasons why Americans could justifiably regard their experiment as something exceptional. As noted in Chapter 3, Jefferson, in particular, assumed that human rights were "natural" and "universal" in character, an assumption that conferred to them their special, inalienable quality. Crucially, Jefferson assumed that property rights were not natural and not universal in character; they were, rather, artificially or socially constructed, making them very much alienable, as rights.

Today, even as we acknowledge that the human rights-oriented purposes of the new republic were operative mainly at the rhetorical level and not fully materialized into law and policy, the preference of Americans to found the purposes of government on the protection of human rights is still something worth remembering today. It is worth remembering because this democratic sensibility, transported into our contemporary historical context, presents a compelling moral and legal justification for

---

[6] The idea that the people themselves were the ultimate authors of the Declaration is strongly reflected in the following works. Pauline Maier, *American Scripture: Making the Declaration of Independence.* New York, NY: Vintage Books, 1997; Danielle Allen, *Our Declaration: A Reading of the Declaration of Independence in Defense of Equality.* New York, NY: W. W. Norton, 2014.

the state's ability to restrict the power of monopolies. And just as we earlier linked the fulfillment of one right, the pursuit of happiness, to the
prohibition of standing armies, Jefferson similarly believed that the fulfillment of the pursuit of happiness depended, among other things, on constitutional restrictions rendering the people free from the consequences
of monopoly power.

On three separate occasions during the years surrounding the Constitutional convention (1787–1789), Jefferson actively campaigned for a
constitutional amendment to restrict monopoly power. Below I bracket
the terminology Jefferson used to formulate his constitutional innovations.

On December 20, 1787, writing to James Madison, Jefferson adopts
the phrase "restriction of monopolies;" on February 7, 1788, to Alexander Donald, he writes "freedom of commerce against monopolies;" a few
days later, on February 12, 1788, to C. F. W. Dumas, he shifts to "no
monopolies in commerce;" and on March 13, 1789, to Francis Hop-
kinson, Jefferson speaks of "freedom from monopolies."[7] Although each
formulation expresses the same basic moral and political principle, I chose
freedom from monopolies for the chapter title because it highlights the
nexus between the formation of unaccountable concentrations of economic power (monopolies), on the one hand, and the consequent restriction this power imposes upon the realm of individual freedom on the
other.

Jefferson's latter formulation permits us to link the freedom of the people, the public happiness of the people, to the people's ability, through the
aegis of a republican state, to restrict these types of economic concentrations. In order to protect the public interest over and against the private
interests of monopolies, then, Jefferson saw his constitutional proposal
as a kind of anti-corruption device. A legal device whose purpose would
be to guard against corruption and other disequalizing consequences that
he assumed would accompany the formation of corporate monopolies.
Alas, Jefferson's proposals to restrict the power of corporate monopolies
weren't constitutionalized during the nation's founding era. However, in

---

[7] These letters can be accessed in https://founders.archives.gov.documents/Jefferson.

subsequent decades and up to the present moment, struggles over the status of monopoly power would intensify across a range of legal, political, and cultural fronts.[8]

"Jump-Starting Democracy": Jefferson's Critique of Aristocratic-Elite Economic and Political Power, 1800–1826

Jefferson's hotly contested, chaotic, yet peaceful election to the presidency in 1800 after three consecutive Federalist-dominated administrations was, for him and his supporters, a very big deal. It ratified in empirical terms the legitimacy of his theory of revolutionary democratic transition. Writing on the subject in retrospect, in 1819, Jefferson declared that "The revolution of 1800 was as real a revolution in the principles of our government, as that of 1776 was in its form."[9] Jefferson wanted Americans to conceptualize this revolution as *real* on moral grounds. To wit: the revolution of 1776 changed the form (or structure) of what had existed, from a loose assemblage of thirteen monarchical dependencies into an independent, formally unified national government. And while this new form of government represented a progressive historical discontinuity, the substantive moral and political principles guiding the *administration of that form* remained almost entirely in the hands of an elite-aristocratic class, on whose behalf the Federalist party was created. Perhaps Joyce Appleby captures the import of this revolution best: "we will lose our grasp of historical reality if we underestimate the power of the aristocratic values that flourished in 1800... we should not forget that Thomas Jefferson jump-started democracy in the United States and, by extension, the world."[10]

From a Jeffersonian perspective, the election of 1800 can be framed as the nation's second moral (interior) revolution, whereby the

---

[8] For a comprehensive history of the American corporation, see Adam Winkler, *We the Corporations: How American Businesses Won Their Civil Rights*. New York: W. W. Norton, 2018.

[9] Thomas Jefferson to Judge Spencer Roane, September 6, 1819.

[10] See, Joyce Appleby, "Thomas Jefferson and the Psychology of Democracy." In *The Revolution of 1800*, eds. James Horn, Jan Ellen Lewis, and Peter S. Onuf. Charlottesville: University of Virginia Press, 2002, 171.

American people peaceably elected to have their republican form administered on the basis of republican values and principles, rather than administered on the basis of elite-aristocratic values and principles. What was most "real" about the revolution of 1800, for Jefferson, then, was that the political body of the nation had morally awakened to the task of consciously rejecting the guiding principles and assumptions of the ruling aristocratic-elite.[11]

Jefferson's post-presidency critique of the ways in which the aristocratic-elites were able to tamp-down on the nation's republican potential make for fascinating reading today. For, just as in Jefferson's time, we can similarly recognize antidemocratic influences operating within the nation's political body, whether the issue is voter suppression or the ideological problem of *Homo Economicus*. In 1816, Jefferson acknowledges the lack of democracy across the country.

> If, then, the control of the people over the organs of their government be the measure of its republicanism, and I confess I know no other measure, it must be agreed that our governments have *much less of republicanism that they ought to have expected*.[12] (my emphasis)

For Jefferson, the stalled political processes he describes did not spring from any lack of such moral capacities within the American people. Instead, Jefferson assigned responsibility for this political downturn to the Federalist party and suggests that they had stymied the nation's republican potential by

> ...a submission of true principle to the influence of European authorities, to speculators on government, whose fears of the people have been inspired by the populace of their own great cities, and were unjustly entertained against the independent, the happy, and therefore the orderly people of the United States.[13]

Jefferson seems emphatic that a demophobic "fear of the people" was not native to the new American political culture, but rather, its presence

---

[11] See, Dan Sisson, *The Revolution of 1800: How Jefferson Rescued Democracy from Tyranny and Faction—And What It Means Today*. Berrett-Koehler, 2013.

[12] Thomas Jefferson to John Taylor, May 28, 1816.

[13] Ibid.

stemmed from the residual ideological strength of Europe's monarchical and aristocratic traditions. During this period, a decade after his own 8-year presidential tenure, Jefferson expresses his well-known hostility to what he considered the historically obsolete values and institutions of the British system. In 1816, he predicts that England's anti-republican tendencies will hopefully lead to that government's downfall:

> It ends, as might have been expected, in the ruin of its people. But this ruin will fall heaviest, as it ought to fall, on that hereditary aristocracy which has for generations been preparing the catastrophe. I hope we shall take warning from the example and crush in its birth the aristocracy of our monied corporations which dare already to challenge our government to a trial of strength and bid defiance to the laws of the country.[14]

At the time that Jefferson articulated his warning about the concentration of corporate power in America, approximately thirty years had elapsed since he initially advocated a constitutional amendment to, in effect, "crush in its birth the aristocracy of our monied corporations." In relation to this missed opportunity, he remarks that, "Much I apprehend that the golden moment may have passed for reforming these heresies."[15] Reading these letters in their historical context, it's obvious that one of the core "heresies" Jefferson is alluding to was the rise of an unaccountable concentration of economic power, something we might accurately call a "corporate monopoly," one that is buttressed today by a doctrine of corporate personhood.

Demystifying the Dogma of Corporate Personhood: A Pedagogical Primer

In the balance of the chapter, I argue that one way to cultivate the moral spirit of Jefferson's constitutional proposal in contemporary educational terms would be for teachers to transform the doctrine of corporate personhood into a site of critical analysis. For the purposes of our inquiry, this doctrine can be seen to symbolize the ultimate political extension of corporate monopoly. Since the doctrine of corporate personhood is

---

[14] Thomas Jefferson to George Logan, November 12, 1816.
[15] Jefferson to John Taylor, May 28, 1816.

most prominently granted legitimacy by the Supreme Court in its *Citizens United* (2010) decision, we need to mount critical investigations of this landmark case. Specifically, we need to inquire into the intersection between law and culture in order to grasp why this doctrine poses such a threat to American democracy. But where to begin? How to frame such a pedagogical intervention?

Let me begin by asserting that the kind of pedagogical approach envisioned here can be justified on the grounds that *Citizens United* has already proven as antidemocratic in the twenty-first century as the *Dred Scott* and *Plessy* decisions proved antidemocratic in the nineteenth and twentieth centuries.[16] Just as *Dred Scott* and *Plessy* codified second-class citizenship for large classifications of Americans in past centuries, *Citizens United* arguably codifies second-class citizenship for the vast majority of Americans today. It achieves this by bequeathing to corporations a civic personhood over and above other citizens by granting to them unparalleled economic power in the electoral arena, powers that normal citizens simply do not have. In this way, the doctrine creates dual and unequal classifications of citizenship. Given our preceding analysis, we may reasonably assume that Jefferson would regard corporate personhood as an oligarchic legal construction, one that must be deemed unconstitutional from the standpoint of a democratic republic.

Moreover, if the normalization of corporate personhood were to become further consolidated, it would carry dangerous implications for the future of both American democracy and our system of public education. It would, for example, not only pose a long-term danger to the moral character of American democracy, but for that reason, it would surely continue to morally erode the very legitimacy of public education as we know it (this theme is further discussed in Chapter 8).

In *Citizens United* and other cases, the Supreme Court strikes down long-standing precedents designed to restrain the inordinate influence of

---

[16]The basis for this assertion is rooted in the following sources, Thom Hartmann, *Unequal Protection: How Corporations Became "People"—And How You Can Fight Back.* San Francisco: Berrett-Koehler Publishers, 2010; Jeffrey Clements, *Corporations Are Not People.* San Francisco: Berrett-Koehler Publishers, 2012; Zephyr Teachout, *Corruption in America: From Benjamin Franklin's Snuff Box to Citizens United.* Cambridge: Harvard University Press, 2016; Sheldon Whitehouse, *Captured: The Corporate Infiltration of American Democracy.* New York, NY: The New Press, 2017.

monied corporations on the political process.[17] It is well-documented that in a post-*Citizens United* America, corporations have been pouring billions of new dollars into the political system. As is also well-documented, corporations do this to alter election outcomes across the country. However, this exercise of corporate muscle is equally as devastating to democratic culture, when it is used to fundamentally shift the terms of public debate. Thus, one of the most ominous cultural consequences of *Citizens United* is that it gives to corporate interests exponentially added powers to shape national conversations over critical issues like climate change, gun control, health care, war, and how to define the purposes of education.

Quite predictably, this pro-corporate trend has intensified economic and political inequalities since it got underway in earnest during the Reagan years. In framing the consequences of *Citizens United*, renowned economist Joseph Stiglitz describes the very patterns of structural inequality that Jefferson's constitutional proposal was designed to prevent: "the rich are getting richer, the richest of the rich are getting still richer, the poor are becoming poorer and more numerous, and the middle class is being hollowed out."[18] On the basis of this brief analysis, it would seem warranted for us to link the doctrine of corporate personhood to both corporate monopoly as well as to these intensifying patterns of inequality.

At this juncture of our analysis, it's relevant to recall that George Counts had identified the antidemocratic consequences of corporate personhood as early as the 1930s (see Chapter 5). Writing as an explicit Jeffersonian in the depths of the Great Depression, Counts argued that the 1886 *Santa Clara Co. v. Pacific Railroad* case symbolized the capitalist/corporate triumph of the "few over the many." Counts identified *Santa Clara* as the legal mechanism by which corporations were recognized as "persons," thereby investing fictional persons with the same individual rights as actual persons. If indeed Counts saw fit nearly a century ago to alert the teachers of the nation to the dangers that corporate personhood posed to American democracy, it would seem justified to alert our students to the same dangers now that they have greatly magnified.

---

[17] See Justice Stevens dissenting opinion in *Citizens United v. Federal Election Commission*, 558 U.S. 310, 2010.

[18] See Joseph Stiglitz, "America's 1 Percent Problem." In *The Price of Inequality: How Today's Divided Society Endangers Our Future*. New York: W. W. Norton, 2013, 1–34.

Several legal scholars and commentators have recently traced the incremental steps by which the doctrine of corporate personhood has been constructed in American jurisprudence. With this backdrop in view, I draw on these and related interpretations to suggest the general outlines of a critical pedagogy for demystifying the dogmas of corporate personhood. Specifically, as a core element of this critical intervention, I examine one crucial moral dimension of the problem that might ordinarily be overlooked: Namely, the fact that corporations, as persons, do not have souls and cannot love.[19]

The pedagogical development of this general philosophical premise—the idea that citizens can be defined by a capacity to love their country—may help to expose, by way of contrast, the limitations and dangers of privileging corporations as rights-bearing citizens. In order to conceptually unpack this approach, then, let's briefly identify some of the conceptual linkages that connect "love" to "citizenship." We can begin by first recognizing the very thing that tends to contradict the moral reciprocity at the center of the love/citizen connection: that is, the problem of corruption.

In Zephyr Teachout's, *Corruption in America*, she traces the concept of corruption as a legal category over the sweep of American history. Teachout observes that the term traditionally referred to elected officials being influenced by powerful private actors to favor their interests over the interests of the public as a whole. And during the founding era, she continues, the word *citizen* was widely understood to denote a public role of the person, with the implication that "a person can take responsibility for a larger political community."[20] The citizen as a social identity thus weds the private individual and her interests with the idea of a larger community and its interests and purposes.

The concept of virtue is also relevant to any discussion of corruption since virtue exists as the polar opposite of corruption. Recall that for Jefferson, virtue as a moral ideal remains incomplete if reduced to its strictly private expressions. By definition, according to this view, both virtue and citizenship require a robust public face as a condition for reaching their fullest potentials. One reason why Jefferson favored the use of state power

[19]On this specific theme, I am indebted to Clements' *Corporations Are Not People*. San Francisco: Berrett-Koehler Publishers, 2012.

[20]Teachout, 236.

to restrict the power of corporate monopolies, was his belief that such centers of power would always attempt to "corrupt" the political process by making it easier for private actors to subvert the larger public interest. Jefferson, in other words, fully appreciated the contradiction between the republic's need to produce virtuous citizens, on the one hand, and the overriding purpose of monopolies, which would always be weighted heavily toward the promotion of private interests.

The rhetoric that corporations are "just like people"—particularly in relation to the Bill of Rights—must be critically interrogated as another crucial step in our pedagogical intervention. This means asking questions about how the corporate form has evolved and manifested itself throughout the nation's history. In this regard, Senator Sheldon Whitehouse has recently argued that the corporate form can and has functioned as a beneficial "economic actor" in the past. This positive contribution must be acknowledged. However, Whitehouse is quick to distinguish this beneficial economic role from the corporation's new role as a "political actor," that is, in its post-*Citizens United* role that, by consolidating corporate political power, practically guarantees to magnify levels of inequality and corruption.[21]

WHO ARE CORPORATIONS?

Who, then, are these corporations that have now garnered first amendment rights? Should we celebrate the extension of such rights to corporations, just as we have celebrated similar extensions to citizens at transformational moments in the nation's history? Should we have a holiday where Americans could commemorate this triumph of corporate rights? Or, alternatively, would it be wiser to interpret this *de jure* extension of individual rights to corporations, as a de facto reduction of the rights of actual citizens?

In order to untangle some of the elusive conceptual connections implicit in the questions posed above, it may be useful to examine the remarkable conceptual linkages that Jefferson makes between virtue, love, and citizenship in a republic.

> Virtue may be defined as the love of the laws and of our country. As such love requires a constant preference of public to private interest, it is the source of all private virtue; for they are nothing more than this very preference itself. Now a government is like everything else: to preserve

[21]Whitehouse, 6.

it we must love it...Everything, therefore, depends on establishing this love in a republic; and to inspire it ought to be the principle business of education.[22]

This amazing passage captures Jefferson's thoughts about what it is, exactly, that lies at the core of citizenship in a republic. Jefferson notes that the kind of love he is talking about in a republic requires "constant preference" of public over private interest. As the "source of all private virtue," the essence of this form of love is embodied in the "very preference itself," that is, love as a desire for something beyond private goods.

It appears, then, that love in this instance—according to Jefferson's notes on the subject—represents the love of certain moral ideals, moral ideals that exist beyond narrower expressions of individual virtue in the private realm. In Teachout's interpretation of this Jeffersonian passage, she observes that, "there is a necessarily intimate emotional role for the state in our hearts. The love must be greater than a mere identification along the lines of nationalism. Instead, the nature of the love must extend to a love of the ideal form of the country."[23] Arguably, this broad conceptual understanding of how love functions in a republic, as a virtuous love of an ideal moral and collective vision, constitutes the moral foundation of citizenship. As a working foundation, then, it would appear to establish a rational basis for disqualifying corporations from being defined as part of We, the People.

Once again, recalling discussions in earlier chapters, we are brought back to Jefferson's repeated statements that it is precisely the Spirit of 76 and its historically rooted moral preferences, or ideals, which he regarded as an expression of a kind of love vital to the future of America's republican experiment.[24] We are on solid ground, therefore, in asserting that Jefferson would regard the doctrine of corporate personhood as a cunning judicial attempt to subvert the Spirit of 76 in the very name of this self-same spirit: "Free Speech for All" declared an oligarchic-friendly majority of the Supreme Court!

---

[22] Thomas Jefferson, *The Commonplace Book*, quoted from Clements, p. 127. This book is apparently a compilation of notes that Jefferson took to summarize his study of various European thinkers.

[23] Teachout, 42.

[24] Peter S. Onuf, "Love and Democracy." https://www.coursera.org/lecture/ageofjefferson/love-and-democracy-t3Hdj.

DISSENTING VOICES AGAINST CORPORATE PERSONHOOD

One of the most eloquent and informed perspectives on the subject of corporate personhood is that of Supreme Court Justice Paul Stevens, whose lengthy dissent in *Citizens United* goes a long distance in demystifying the dogma of corporate personhood. He comments:

> It might also be added that corporations have no consciences, no beliefs, no feelings, no thoughts, no desires. Corporations help structure and facilitate the activities of human beings, to be sure, and their "personhood" often serves as a useful legal fiction. But they are not themselves members of "We the People" by whom and for whom our Constitution was established... The Court's blinkered and aphoristic approach to the First Amendment may well promote corporate power at the cost of the individual and collective self-expression the Amendment was meant to serve. It will undoubtedly cripple the ability of ordinary citizens, Congress, and the States to adopt even limited measures to protect against corporate domination of the electoral process. Americans may be forgiven if they do not feel the Court has advanced the cause of self-government today.[25]

Indeed, if we look at the most powerful corporations, the global multinationals, it's quite obvious that unlike Jefferson's image of a virtuous citizen, corporations do not and cannot "love" any country. Jefferson stressed that "everything depends" on establishing this love in a republic, and in the absence of such love no republic could long exist. The constant preference of today's corporate monopolies—from Exxon and Facebook to Amazon and Pearson—is above all for profit and private interest. In a capitalist economy, of course, corporations naturally pursue profit making. However, the problem here, which Jefferson foresaw and which today is more obvious than ever, is that corporations seek to define themselves not just as artificial persons for reasons of legal expedience, but as acting citizens for reasons of political dominance. This analytical distinction is vital. Our recognition of it would seem to preclude corporations from qualifying as actual citizens, precisely because they lack the capacity to love their country, or, to paraphrase Justice Stevens, they are a category that should never be considered part of We, the People.

Just as Clements and Stevens want readers to recognize the crucial fact that corporations should not be viewed as real citizens, constitutional

---

[25] Stevens, *Citizens United*, 558 U.S. 310, 2010.

scholar Ciara Torres-Spelliscy, similarly attempts to undermine the legitimacy of corporate personhood by identifying the corporation's lack of soul. It is noteworthy, I think, that these three constitutional scholars—Stevens, Clement, and Torres-Spelliscy—rest much of their arguments against corporate personhood on the related claims that corporations are soulless and cannot love.

Torres-Spelliscy, perhaps inspired by Stevens dissent, pierces the deceptively innocent conceits sequestered within the notion of corporate personhood:

> There are absurdities that flow from granting legal fictions Constitutional rights that were intended for humans. Corporations don't have minds, and without one it is hard to see how a corporation "thinks" about any political issue du jour from gay rights to the budget deficit. Without a soul, it's hard to conceptualize how a corporation could "believe" in anything whether it is transubstantiation of communion or the morality of birth control.[26] (Brennan Center for Justice)

Echoing Steven's dissent, Torres-Spelliscy points out that the majority in *Citizens United* treats corporations as if they have a mind, as if they can actually believe in certain political values, and on this basis they can "vote" by spending billions of dollars (without any disclosure) on those issues they "believe" in. In considering the perspectives of these dissenting voices, including that of George Counts, we have a persuasive set of arguments for pedagogically resisting the doctrine of corporate personhood. Among other things, the inquiry suggests that democratic-minded teachers searching for ways to demystify the dogmas of this antidemocratic legal doctrine might well begin by fleshing-out, conceptually, love's relation to citizenship. In focusing attention on this underlying experiential dimension, as that which ultimately transforms formal citizens into actually embodied citizens, we can position our students to grasp both the deeper emotional layers of citizenship and the absurdity of normalizing corporate personhood as a legitimate extension of citizenship.

Finally, in conclusion, it may be productive to review the language of a recently proposed Constitutional amendment designed to abolish corporate personhood. We have good reason to believe that Jefferson would

---

[26]Ciara Torres-Spelliscy, "The History of Corporate Personhood." https:// Brennancenter.org. April 7, 2014.

endorse the following updated version of his proposal to secure freedom from monopolies. The text of "The People's Rights Amendment" identifies one of the most urgent contemporary needs of the republic—at least from a Jeffersonian perspective. While educators cannot bring about the end of corporate personhood by ourselves without working in solidarity with a range of social movements, we can nonetheless contribute to these movements by developing robust ways to deconstruct the doctrine of corporate personhood within the nation's classrooms.

THE PEOPLE'S RIGHTS AMENDMENT (XXVIII)

Section I. We the people who ordain and establish this Constitution intend the rights protected by this Constitution to be the rights of natural persons.

Section II. The words people, person, or citizen as used in the Constitution do not include corporations, limited liability companies, or other corporate entities established by the laws of any state, the United States, or any foreign state. Such corporate entities are subject to any regulation as the people, through their elected state and federal representatives, deem reasonable and are as otherwise consistent with the powers of Congress and the States under this Constitution.

Section III. Nothing contained herein shall be construed to limit the people's rights of freedom of speech, freedom of the press, free exercise of religion, and all such other rights of the people, which rights are inalienable.[27]

---

[27] As quoted in Clements, 166.

CHAPTER 8

An Education Amendment

OVERVIEW

Today it is a seldom-appreciated fact that on two occasions—once in 1782 and again in 1806—Jefferson wrote about constitutionalizing a legal right to public education. Jefferson's first mention of such a constitutional renovation was intended for inclusion in Virginia's state constitution, while the second, more extended discussion, was intended for inclusion in the federal constitution. Although these attempts to elevate the status of education to that of a constitutionally protected legal right never materialized at either level of government during Jefferson's lifetime, they are well worth recalling today.

By revisiting these nearly forgotten proposals with a receptive eye, we can open ourselves to the possibility of encountering valuable insights from unsuspected places. To begin with, both proposals remind us of the underlying moral vision of education that must be central to any polity that identifies itself as democratic. The 1806 proposal, significantly, expresses Jefferson's foundational belief that if public education was to be properly valued in the new nation, and if its role in forming an intelligent citizenry was to be properly valued, it should be enshrined as a constitutionally protected federal right. Unfortunately, Jefferson does not tell us a great deal about what it would mean to make public education a federally protected legal right. Unlike other pieces of educational legislation that Jefferson authored, such as *A Bill for the More General Diffusion of*

© The Author(s) 2020
K. T. Burch, *Jefferson's Revolutionary Theory and the Reconstruction of Educational Purpose*, The Cultural and Social Foundations of Education, https://doi.org/10.1007/978-3-030-45763-1_8

Knowledge, his written remarks on the subject of constitutionalizing education are frustratingly short on details.

The first broad aim of the chapter will be to recover a sense of the revolutionary implications and moral spirit underlying Jefferson's constitutional proposals. Proceeding on this basis, and taking into consideration the current neoliberal trends in education, the second broad aim will be to argue that the need for making public education a federally protected legal right is perhaps greater today than ever before.[1] In this endeavor, Jefferson should be recruited as a powerful ally.

HISTORICAL CONTEXT

Jefferson initially broaches the subject of an education amendment in his *Notes on the State of Virginia* (1787). In Query XIV he asserts that,

> Every government degenerates when trusted to the rulers of the people alone. The people themselves are its only safe depositories. And to render them safe, their minds must be improved to a certain degree…An amendment of our constitution must here come in aid of the public education.[2]

In articulating what are by now familiar themes, Jefferson connects the need for an education amendment to the imperative of enabling ordinary people to participate more readily and intelligently in the activities of self-government. "The influence over government," he insists, "must be shared among all the people."[3] A review of the conceptual sequencing of the education passages in Query XIV reveals a direct correspondence in Jefferson's thinking between the need for extending suffrage so as to restrain corruption, and the need for a right to education so as to establish the conditions in which the American people might exercise their citizenship more intelligently.

The nexus between voting, education, and anti-republican corruption is nicely summarized when Jefferson states that, "…it has been thought

---

[1] For a superb and eminently teachable account of why education should be constitutionalized at the federal level, see Stephen Lurie, "Why Doesn't the Constitution Guarantee the Right to Education?" *The Atlantic*, October 16, 2013.

[2] Thomas Jefferson, "Notes on the State of Virginia, Query XIV." In *Thomas Jefferson: Writings*. New York: The Library of America, 1984, 274.

[3] Ibid., 274.

that corruption is restrained by confining the right of suffrage to a few of the wealthier people: but it would be more effectually restrained by an *extension of that right* to such numbers as would bid defiance to the means of corruption" (my emphasis).[4] Indeed, it would be spectacularly inconsistent for Jefferson to propose an extension of voting rights without taking care, at the same time, to invent supportive public institutions, such as free public schools, whose explicit aim would be to cultivate the American people's potential as citizens.

Writing decades later as the nation's third president, Jefferson uses his second State of the Union address (1806) to propose an education amendment to the US Constitution.[5] Specifically, he promotes the idea of adapting what he called a "national establishment for education." I say *idea* because in reading these passages, it's hard to grasp what exactly Jefferson had in mind in proposing this constitutional amendment, as he leaves a lot unspecified about the substance of his proposal. Notably, Jefferson does not furnish readers with a draft of how the language of such an amendment might "read" as constitutional text. In choosing not to include this rather crucial element, perhaps he expected that the language of the amendment could be ironed out later. And, while the text of the State of the Union proposal does not state explicitly that the amendment was intended to form a federal university, most scholars agree that this is what Jefferson was discussing. The language Jefferson uses to describe his education amendment is so ambiguous that it's both inviting and frustrating at once. In any event, at the conclusion of the chapter, I propose a Jeffersonian-oriented draft of a federal education amendment.

Jefferson raises the subject of a constitutional "establishment for public education" in the larger context of the fiscal shape of the union. Jefferson proudly reports the nation was running surpluses, cutting military expenditures, and the large debt inherited from previous Federalist administrations had been virtually eliminated. The happy fiscal environment that Jefferson sketches permits him to turn toward the future and propose a set of internal, public improvements. In this regard, it is worth emphasizing that Jefferson categorizes "public education" as one component of a

---

[4] Ibid., 275.

[5] Thomas Jefferson to Congress, December 2, 1806, Draft of Message to Congress. In *The Works of Thomas Jefferson in Twelve Volumes*. Federal Edition. Collected and Edited by Paul Leicester Ford. http://www.loc.gov/resource/mtj1.037_0012_0030.

set of "public improvements," discussed alongside roads, bridges, canals, and other infrastructure of vital national interest.[6]

With these fiscal conditions in view, Jefferson proceeds to think through the various challenges facing the future status of education in American society. In reviewing the relevant passages, he appears to be asking the nation to think about the institution of education in two fundamentally new ways. First, in a legal sense, as a constitutional amendment; and secondly, in a related economic sense, as an institution that could be enduringly financed through the sale of public lands. On this latter point, we do know that the policy of financing public education through the sale of federal lands initially found expression within the group of laws referred to as the Northwest Ordinances (1792).[7] Since Jefferson was directly involved in drafting many of these statutes, his State of the Union proposal represents an extension of the historically novel policy of educational institution-making through state-sponsored land grants.

Despite the considerable ambiguity that surrounds Jefferson's second call for an education amendment, he still manages to offer some fascinating insights into how the nation might secure a durable source of income to support the amendment he envisions.

> I suppose an amendment to the Constitution, by consent of the States, necessary, because the objects now recommended are not among those enumerated in the Constitution, and to which it permits the public moneys to be applied.
>
> The present consideration of a national establishment for education particularly is rendered proper by this circumstance also, that if Congress, approving the proposition, shall yet think it more eligible to found it on a donation of lands, they have it now in their power to endow it with those which will be among the earliest to produce the necessary income. This foundation would have the advantage of being independent of war, which may suspend other improvements by requiring for its own purposes the resources destined for them.[8]

---

[6] Ibid.

[7] Paul Mattingly and Edward Stevens, Jr., eds., *"...Schools and the Means of Education Shall Forever Be Encouraged": A History of Education in the Old Northwest, 1887–1880.*

[8] TJ, State of Union, 1806.

Jefferson foresees that without a "foundation" of income to adequately fund a national establishment for education, any institution-building in this regard would constantly be in jeopardy of having its resources diverted to more pressing concerns, such as war and military expenditures. It would seem that Jefferson wanted to constitutionalize public education at the national level, in large part, because he believed that this constitutional elevation would render education "independent of war" from an economic standpoint. Rendering public education independent of war thus emerges as a kind of unsuspected political problem and policy challenge that Jefferson shrewdly anticipates and seeks to remedy with his constitutional proposal. In making an explicit connection between the funding of public education and the expected threat posed to it by policies of constant war, Jefferson declares:

> Were armies to be raised whenever a speck of war is on the horizon, we never should have been without them. Our resources would have been exhausted on dangers which have never happened, instead of being reserved for what is really to take place.[9]

Readers may well marvel at Jefferson's prescient political analysis. Nor should it be difficult for us to see in Jefferson's words a mirror image of America's current budgetary priorities, whereby resources for education and public improvements have become "suspended" and "exhausted" over permanently imagined enemies and "dangers which have never happened." From where we sit today, it would appear that public education, rather than being an institution whose foundation is independent of war, seems instead to have evolved, or should we say, devolved, into a very dependent institution—dependent upon the political economy of America's permanent warfare state.

HISTORICIZING JEFFERSON'S CORE INSIGHT AS A TOOL OF CRITICAL ANALYSIS

To begin to frame Jefferson's core insight as a tool of critical analysis, we need to recall that, in Chapter 6, Martin Luther King affirms the substance of this insight in his later writings and speeches. King does this by identifying a prime structural feature of the nation's political economy: a

[9] Ibid.

relational condition in which the diversion of resources from education and other life-affirming policies are interpreted to be that which enabled, and still enables, America's massive military expenditures. In a sense, then, by juxtaposing expenditures for war with the relative lack of expenditures for education and other health-related national interests, King provides an historical update to Jefferson's original insight. Equally instructive perhaps is how King's critical analysis provides a rather telling index of our national values and priorities. Much like Jefferson, then, King expresses a deep concern about the dire consequences that would necessarily accompany the formation of an overly militarized national identity.

In so cogently identifying a direct economic and political relation between these two competing institutional establishments—war and education—Jefferson seems to argue that constitutionalizing public education would have the advantage of more firmly embedding this emergent institution within American society. Moreover, it appears that Jefferson's plan to constitutionalize education and to finance it based on a land-grant formula—independent of war—was all about devising a way to protect the economic and moral status of public education from the bottomless appetites of America's reigning war parties and allied institutions. Jefferson emphatically warns the American people that powerful interests would always invent reasons for war, always clamor for military expenditures "whenever a speck of war is on the horizon," and therefore would always articulate new objects of enmity around which to organize an increasingly militarized national identity.

In crucial ways, then, as we saw in Chapter 7, Jefferson's remarks presage Eisenhower's farewell address (1961) in which Ike warned about the "unwarranted influence" that the "military-industrial complex" would have on diminishing the democratic spirit of the country.[10] In an earlier speech (1953), Eisenhower expressed the same general *relational condition* that Jefferson and King both understood when he wrote: "Every gun that is made, every warship launched, every rocket fired signifies, in a final sense, a theft from those who hunger and are not fed, those who are cold

---

[10]For a recent in-depth analysis of Eisenhower's speech, see James Ledbetter, *Unwarranted Influence: Dwight D. Eisenhower and the Military-Industrial Complex.* New Haven: Yale University Press, 2011.

and are not clothed...The cost of one heavy bomber is this: a modern brick school in more than 30 cities."[11]

What I am calling Jefferson's "core political insight"—the economic, political, and moral tensions that connect the institution of education to that of war—should be framed today as a valuable resource and tool of critical analysis. As such, this mode of interpretation could serve as a theoretical aperture for revealing an empirically verifiable snapshot of the national values profile, as that profile is reflected in the federal budget.[12] If we frame Jefferson's insight as a heuristic device in this manner, we can position ourselves to interrogate a set of asymmetrical power and value relations that often elude conventional modes of critique and categories of analysis.

Applied to today's classroom, for example, students might learn to see that the structural inequalities that lead to so many inequalities in educational outcome, can now be interpreted, on solid epistemic grounds, as a kind of institutional pattern caused by the nation's trillion-dollar Pentagon budgets. Discussions about the nature of this "cause and effect" relationship (high military expenditures = low education expenditures), would likely stimulate students' capacity for thinking more deeply about the underlying conflicts in value that *inform* the formation of American identity. As a tool of interpretation, then, the paradoxical and conflictual relationship that Jefferson identifies between military power and values, on the one hand, and the power and values of education on the other, could be used to encourage students to form new questions about the conflicts in power and values pulsating within the national identity formation. Among other questions, such inquiries may prompt students to ask: *Who are We, and, what do We become, when vast resources are devoted to technologies of war and such meager resources to education?*

If I am not mistaken, then, we should corral Jefferson's and King's core political insights into a generalized concept and deploy it for the purpose of forming new questions about existing power relations in the United States. Any serious review of power relations in the United States would also show how these contests waged over the formation of national values and identity, have never been conducted on an even playing field,

---

[11] Ibid., pp. 2, 8. As Ledbetter asserts, Ike's 1953 "Chance for Peace" speech had a "dramatic worldwide impact."

[12] Costs of War Project, Watson Institute, International & Public Affairs, Brown University. https://watson.brown.edu/costsofwar.

so to speak. Indeed, it was arguably for this reason that Jefferson wished to constitutionalize public education—to help even an uneven playing field. For explicit in Jefferson's text on the subject, there is a recognition that because military power seemed to constitute an institutional given in comparison to education, the exercise of that already existing power would give the military establishment an unequal advantage in its ability to shape the formation of national values according to its own interests. Under this scenario, Jefferson foresaw that the nascent institution of public education would very likely never achieve the kind of independent status it deserved.

A Philosophical Justification for an Education Amendment

From Jefferson's perspective, the country's ongoing failure to constitutionalize a civic-purposed and durably financed system of public education would have serious anti-revolutionary consequences. In one crucial respect, the failure to elevate public education to the status of a constitutional right would tend to erode the integrity of other foundational democratic moral ideals—such as encouraging a "mass diffusion of knowledge" among the people, or of using the positive power of the state to promote intergenerational "crusades against ignorance." For Jefferson, any diminution of these enlightenment-oriented moral ideals would undermine the healthy development of American democracy. More positively, on the other hand, the eventual constitutionalization of these enlightenment purposes (in theory at least) would have the effect of mobilizing and bringing into being the experiential stuff of the revolutionary process, defined here as personal enactments toward participatory readiness and democratic cultural life.

Jefferson's proposals to constitutionalize public education also expressed his desire to enshrine into law a philosophical, moral, and political proposition close to his heart—the legitimacy of the enlightenment assumption of human educability. Indeed, the prospect that the American people might transition toward deeper levels of democratization relies in part on the truth-value accorded to this foundational assumption. Therefore, it would not be an exaggeration to say that, for Jefferson, the absence of a constitutional right to a civic-purposed and independently

financed public education, could only mean that the progressive formation of an ever-broadening public intelligence—upon which much of his
revolutionary theory depended—would be fatally compromised.

Today, in addition to our failure to protect public education through a
constitutional amendment, we can identify another immediate danger facing American public education. This danger manifests itself in the privatization movement in education, a neoliberal reform whose stated purposes
clearly preclude any possibility that the status of public education might
be affirmed through constitutional amendment. Let us now turn briefly
to examine at least two ways in which the privatization movement in education works to eviscerate the democratic heart of Jefferson's educational
vision.

APOCALYPSE NOW! A JEFFERSONIAN GLIMPSE
AT THE PRIVATIZATION MOVEMENT IN EDUCATION

What is most striking about the policy aims of today's privatization movement in education, is that, taken as a whole, they contradict the main
tenets of Jefferson's vision of public education—and do so in consequential ways.

It is easy to say that Jefferson would wince at the thought of Betsy De
Voss serving as the nation's secretary of education. It's also easy to say
that Jefferson would frame De Voss as a billionaire, potential destroyer
of public education and of the wall separating the church/state/school
relation. Jefferson would probably add that, historically speaking, the privatization movement in education could be designated as *neo-colonial* in
relation to how its purposes are defined. In this regard, it's worth recalling that, in a pre-1776 historical context, institutionalized education for
colonial youth was sporadic and overwhelmingly private and religious in
character. Its private and religious character, moreover, was anchored in
an aristocratic/elitist political economy that catered primarily to the children of the rich.[13]

To explain how these neocolonial policies function as both symbol and
reality of the nation's moral and political regression, I offer a Jeffersonian

---

[13] See Johann Neem, *Democracy's Schools: The Rise of Public Education*. Philadelphia:
Johns Hopkins University Press, 2017.

interpretation of two signature policy initiatives of the privatization movement. In the first place, we shall consider the question of who controls
the governance of schools, and secondly, what "school choice" means in
relation to Jefferson's democratic model of school governance.

As previously established in Chapter 3, one of the most democratic and
radical dimensions of Jefferson's Bill No. 79, was the organization of its
bureaucratic structure. Jefferson took great care to design a highly decentralized form of school governance, a framework that would administer
the schools on the basis of democratic standards of equality, accountability, and civic participation. Bill No. 79 exhaustively details the minutia
of these open, democratic procedures. Not only did Jefferson want the
schools to be based on principles of democratic governance, his educational legislation also envisioned the construction of institutional bridges
between locally controlled school systems (called hundreds) and locally
controlled political units (called wards). Jefferson theorized that a grass-
roots arrangement linking the schools to the broader political ward system
would encourage citizens to transcend the timid and procedural practices
of citizenship ordained within the US Constitution. At least in theory,
the ward system and the hundreds system, when acting in concert, were
understood to serve as so many institutional bridges that would connect
local schools to civic participation and to ever broader levels of civic and
political engagement.

In brazen disregard of Jefferson's democratized blueprint for public
school governance, the privatization and charter school movement today
works powerfully against the principle of local control of schools. Diane
Ravitch, for one, explains that when charter schools are challenged in
court to submit to independent audits, their legal teams reply there is no
requirement for corporate-constituted educational institutions to comply
with public and democratic norms of transparency and accountability.[14]
This privacy claim, which charter schools as corporate entities have a legal
right to assert, means however, that their budgets, their internal communications, their hiring and firing procedures, and all other forms of
decision-making within the schools, are effectively shielded from public
scrutiny. While the assertion of this corporate right is indeed legal, the
broadening application of this principle, particularly when undertaken to

[14] Diane Ravitch, "Protect Democratic Control of Public Schools." In *Reign of Error: The Hoax of the Privatization Movement and the Danger to America's Public Schools*. New York: Alfred A. Knopf, 2013, 278–289.

conceal the inner-workings of the nation's schools from norms of public accountability, represents a giant leap backward from a Jeffersonian perspective. Corporate and religious control of school governance is exactly what Jefferson's legislative reforms were intended to transcend and guard against.

Another tenet of the privatization movement is that "school choice" can and should function as a vehicle to dismantle public education as we know it. The proponents of school choice tout this principle as part of a seamless ideological weave of an ever-expanding consumer imaginary. Just as consumers can choose from among a cornucopia of products, the advocates of privatization maintain that students, as neo-customers, should be able to exercise their "freedom" to choose which school they wish to attend. However, there's scant evidence to suggest that the hedge-fund champions of school choice give much thought to the effects these policies have had, or might have, on actually existing communities—communities whose centers of gravity often revolve around their local public schools. Ravitch offers a stinging rebuke to this neoliberal narrative:

> As school choice becomes the basis for public policy, the school becomes not a community institution but an institution that meets the needs of its customers. The school reaches across district lines to find customers; it markets its offerings to potential students. Districts poach students from each other, in hopes of getting more dollars. The customers choose or reject the school, as they would choose or reject a restaurant; it's their choice. The community no longer feels any ties to the school, because the school is not part of the community.[15]

Countless neighborhoods across the country have witnessed the meaningful ties that once connected them organically to their community schools, rudely usurped by the implementation of school choice policies. Ravitch's indictment of the privatization movement in education exposes the full scope of its antidemocratic agenda. For the purposes of this book, I hope that this brief glimpse of the privatization movement's signature policies, at least begins to indicate how they directly contradict the moral and political foundations of Jefferson's educational vision: that of a secular, democratically organized system of free and equal, civic-purposed, locally governed public schools.

[15] Ibid., 312.

DUSTING-OFF THE GUARANTEE CLAUSE FOR THE PURPOSE OF CONSTITUTIONALIZING A FEDERAL RIGHT TO PUBLIC EDUCATION

In this final section of the chapter, I argue that the guarantee clause of the US Constitution (Article IV, Section IV) should be recruited to bolster efforts to constitutionalize a federal right to education. The guarantee clause stipulates that the Constitution shall "guarantee to every state in the union, a republican form of government," a guarantee that includes protecting member states against "invasion" and "domestic violence."[16]

The argument here is straightforward. It rests on the assumption that an indivisible correspondence exists between the identity of the state and the identity of that state's educational purposes. We can begin to approximate the meaning of this indivisible correspondence by examining the following proposition.

If the Constitution guarantees a republican form of government to every state in the union, it would seem to follow that if any state government were to allow the civic purposes of its public schools to fundamentally deteriorate, such deterioration over time would pose an existential threat to the identity of that state's republican form of government. At least based on Jefferson's educational thought and affirmed by other educational thinkers in the early republic, we are on safe ground to assert the factual correctness—the truth—of perceiving an indivisible correspondence between the ideological character of a state and the ideological character and purposes of that state's educational institutions.

Significantly, in this regard, recently filed federal litigation invokes the guarantee clause to support the claim of a federal right to a civic-purposed form of public education. In *Cook v. Raimondo* 1:18 US-cv-00645 (2018),[17] attorney and educational scholar, Michael Rebell, contends that the state of Rhode Island is currently in violation of the guarantee clause (among other constitutional provisions) because the state is failing to provide a decent—or any—civic education to its students. According to Rebell's arguments, this official state neglect has had the

---

[16] U.S. Constitution, Article 4, Section 4. In *The Declaration of Independence and the Constitution of the United States*, ed. Pauline Maier. New York: Bantam Classics, 1998.

[17] *Cook v. Raimondo* (2018) 1:18 US-cv-645. United States District Court, District of Rhode Island.

demonstrable effect of impairing the formation of viable democratic civic identities among whole classes of young citizens in Rhode Island:

> Defendants have violated the Republican Guarantee Clause of Article Four, Section Four of the United States Constitution by failing to provide the individual named plaintiffs and other members of the plaintiff class a meaningful opportunity to obtain an education adequate to prepare them to be capable voters and jurors, to exercise effectively their right of free speech and other constitutional rights, to participate effectively and intelligently in our open political system and to function productively *as civic participants capable of maintaining a republic form of government.*[18] (my emphasis)

I emphasize the last sentence because it affirms the validity of the "indivisible correspondence" between the identity of a state and the necessary role that education must play in reproducing—maintaining—that state's identity. It should be duly noted that Rebell's argument rests on a proposition that was not only accepted by educational thinkers in the early republic, as previously mentioned, but also by a long tradition of federal case law in relation to education. Namely, that the purposes of public education must be defined as civic and specifically republican in character so that the states' systems of education can fulfill their roles in forming republican citizens and thereby maintaining the republic itself.[19]

It is true that Jefferson never mentions the guarantee clause in relation to his proposal for adding an educational amendment to the US Constitution. However, as was discussed in the previous section, if Jefferson were around today to witness the neocolonial ascendance of an oligarchic-led privatization movement in public education, he would probably be among the first to metaphorically "dust-off" the guarantee clause and use it as a constitutional basis for legitimizing a federal right to education. To further pursue this line of inquiry, let's examine the full text of Article IV, Section IV:

---

[18] Ibid., 44–45.

[19] For the purposes of this book, it is critical to recognize that state and federal judiciaries have defined the civic purposes of public education as foundational. Michael Rebell's, *Flunking Democracy* may well be the best contemporary account of the history of this principle. While the Brown v. Topeka Board of Education, Yoder v. Wisconsin and San Antonio v Rodriguez cases, among others, recognize the civic purposes of public education as foundational, the courts have yet to sufficiently enforce this normative assertion through law.

> The United States shall guarantee to every State in this Union a Republican Form of Government, and shall protect each of them against Invasion; and on Application of the Legislature, or of the Executive (when the Legislature cannot be convened), against domestic Violence.[20]

In effect, then, Rebell's litigation requests that the federal government act upon its "implied power" to guarantee not only the republican character of its state governments in a *physical* sense, but also to guarantee the republican character of its public schools in a deeper *moral* sense. Thus, the "correspondence" between the state and its schools can be interpreted as "indivisible" owing to this crucial binding moral element. Rebell's litigation petitions the court to recognize that if any state's educational system is determined to be non-civic or anti-republican in purpose, those state's should be compelled by the US Constitution to realign their educational purposes in a manner consistent with the guarantee clause (including the equal protection clause of the Fourteenth amendment).

If we were to continue to interpret the text of the guarantee clause along these lines, particularly given the ascendant power of the privatization movement in education, we might further observe that the identity of public education today is threatened by a well-financed "Invasion" of corporate mercenaries. This hostile takeover and occupation has transformed thousands of previously public spaces into private, corporate spaces, a process that arguably constitutes a form of "domestic Violence" against the republican character of one of the states' premier identity-forming institutions. Moreover, the process of stripping civic education and the humanities from the curriculum as part of monetizing the schools—that is, of viewing them as new zones for profit-seeking—could similarly be said to constitute a form of "domestic Violence" against the republican character of one of the states' premier identity-forming institutions.

All of this raises an unavoidable question: How long can we continue to exist as a "democratic republic" while the purposes of our public schools are increasingly dominated by oligarchic interests and purposes? Faced, it seems, with two starkly different educational futures, perhaps Americans need to recognize that Jefferson was right in at least one respect—that the best and most enduring way to protect and preserve

---

[20] U.S. Constitution, Article 4, Section 4.

the independence of public education is through a constitutional amendment to the US Constitution.[21]

Proposal for a 28th Amendment to the US Constitution

Section 1. In order to secure the future of the republic, all minor citizens shall enjoy the human right to a civic-purposed public education of equal high quality.

Section 2. a Funding for the implementation and enforcement of this right shall be derived, in part, from subtracting 10% per annum from total discretionary defense expenditures for use in the United States Department of Education.

b. Funding for the implementation and enforcement of this right shall be derived, in part, from federally held landholdings whose assets can be used to promote the general welfare.

Section 3. A national education committee shall be formed of 11 members whose mandate will be to provide curricular guidance and direct economic resources to enhance the schools' ability to carry out their foundational civic-based purposes enumerated in Section 1.

> **a:** Membership of the committee shall be appointed by the Secretary of Education and serve for a maximum of 6 years.
>
> **b:** An annual report regarding the educational state of the nation shall be issued on the first day of September of each year.

Section 4. Congress shall have the power to enforce and implement these articles by appropriate legislation.

---

[21] For a strong argument for constitutionalizing education at the federal level, see The Southern Education Project, "No Time to Lose: Why America Needs an Education Amendment to the US Constitution to Improve Public Education." http://www.southerneducation.org.

PART III

Renewal: Reconstructing Educational Purpose

CHAPTER 9

Crystallizing the Educational Implications of Jefferson's Revolutionary Theory

Based on discussions in previous chapters, we can identify three core elements that provide Jefferson's theory with its essential form and substance. (1) The revisionary element, (2) the dissent element, and (3) the theory's function as a rhetorical device to channel the philosophical and moral principles of the Spirit of 76. The aim of this chapter is to crystallize the manner in which these elements might fit together conceptually and normatively within contemporary classrooms.

By first bracketing and fleshing out the defining elements of Jefferson's revolutionary theory in this chapter, we position ourselves in the final two chapters to apply this broad conceptual framing to the task of radically rethinking the purposes of today's curriculum. In Chapter 10, for example, three of Jefferson's most radical moral propositions are framed as a foundational basis for justifying the reconstruction of educational purposes, purposes that will be identified and further articulated in Chapter 11 under the rubric of what I am calling a K-12 Curricular Redesign. The point of this latter exercise will be to provide three snapshots of new directions in curricular purpose, so that today's curriculum can better meet the needs of a new generation of Americans. Consistent with the Renewal motif of Part III, then, the final two chapters reflect distinct yet related thought experiments regarding the ways in which Jefferson's revolutionary theory can be utilized at this historical moment to aid in the reconstruction of the democratic moral purposes of public education.

© The Author(s) 2020   143
K. T. Burch, *Jefferson's Revolutionary Theory and the Reconstruction of Educational Purpose*, The Cultural and Social Foundations of Education, https://doi.org/10.1007/978-3-030-45763-1_9

THE CAPACITY AND WILLINGNESS TO REVISE

As we saw in Chapter 3, Jefferson's revolutionary theory was predicated on a belief in the human capacity and willingness to revise. The capacity to revise (to unlearn and relearn), as part of the human inheritance, gives to Jefferson's theory its hopeful quality that things can change for the better, that the moral progress of humankind, while obviously never something easily achieved, at least provides some basis for believing that the transformation of both individuals and cultures is possible.

Moreover, it bears repeating that merely recognizing the capacity to revise in no way guarantees that individuals or cultures will be motivated to actualize this defining human characteristic. The individuals' moral or ethical *willingness* to fulfill this human capacity, as an ethical ideal, is equally important for our purposes, as the capacity to revise means virtually nothing without the development of a desire or willingness *to* revise. Put differently, assuming the capacity to revise is intrinsic to all human beings, we don't have to "do" anything to prompt it into existence. On the other hand, the *willingness* to revise, because it is the result of an ethical choice made by individuals, is the more challenging component since the intention to revise and to act is something that must be cultivated into existence. As we recognize the fundamental pedagogical dimension of this cardinal Jeffersonian virtue, a bevy of questions spring up in relation to what educators could do within their respective disciplinary locations to nurture this revisionary quality in their classrooms. Perhaps one important principle to bear in mind with regard to human capacities in general, is that, as capacities, they are best exercised through an educational process of drawing out rather than through a process of depositing information. The indispensability of the process of drawing out to the related domains of civic education, philosophy, and the humanities will be further underscored in the following chapters.

It cannot be overstated that Jefferson's revolutionary theory is anchored in the recognition that as historical conditions change, human needs will inevitably change as well. The formation of a civic identity capable of keeping pace with and addressing these changes in human needs was perhaps the most hoped-for outcome underlying Jefferson's theory. Particularly in light of Chapter 3, we would be justified in interpreting this revisionary quality of Jefferson's theory as foundational to democratic culture and education. Among other things, Jefferson's theory alerts us to the fact that one of the chief tasks of democracy is to produce citizens who can respond creatively both to the inevitable evolution of human needs and to *ideas* about how those evolving needs, as problems, might be remedied. Once again, we are reminded that members of democratic regimes will always need to have their abilities for self-critique and revision well developed. In this regard, we have seen how Allen's concept of participatory readiness closely aligns with what Jefferson envisioned as the gold standard of democratic citizenship. As noted in earlier chapters, the aim of exercising and cultivating capabilities for participatory readiness would create citizens not only more awake to the democratic values, but equally important, such an education would create citizens ethically poised to act on behalf of the democratic values.

EDUCATING FOR DISSENT AS A HUMAN RIGHT

The dissent element of Jefferson's theory refers not only to the need to value dissent, but also to something beyond that—the right to an education for dissent. This Jeffersonian-inspired proposition may sound like a radical idea. However, it is common for schools to adopt curricula intended to foster the intelligent exercise of constitutionally enumerated rights. For example, students learn to read, to write, to speak, to examine history for present-day lessons, and sometimes to debate contemporary moral controversies. The normative aim of these laudable classroom activities is to cultivate within the young values and sensibilities necessary for the meaningful exercise of their constitutional rights and responsibilities. This would include, among other things, casting intelligent votes, exercising one's freedom of speech, serving on a jury, keeping abreast of public affairs, and participating in multiple sites of civil society. Yet, how often do the schools give serious heed to the explicit aim of developing those values and sensibilities that would enable the meaningful exercise of our "dissent-oriented" constitutional rights? Probably not often enough.

In reply to this problem, let us recall that Jefferson's Bill No. 79, while affirming the fundamental civic purpose of education, includes a direct reference to education's role in bringing about intelligent forms of dissent (as an informed civic action). As Chapter 3 highlights, not only are citizens to be educated to know tyranny and ambition in all its forms (acquiring political knowledge), but that Jefferson also talked about educating the young in an ethical sense (what we have identified as a sense of participatory readiness). In Jefferson's view, once the young are equipped with an understanding of the nation's political tradition and its values, they would likely be "prompt to exert their powers against" any anti-republican tendencies whenever and wherever they perceived them.

It is thus remarkable that one of the purposes of public education as Jefferson envisioned it was to develop in students' their abilities for civic action. It's remarkable because within the logic of today's sterile and amoralized neoliberal paradigm of education, the reigning illusion seems to be that a politically "neutral" education is possible and desirable. In stark contrast to this deceptive neoliberal illusion, Jefferson believed that schools ought to provide students with a political and moral education for intelligent dissent; otherwise, both individual and cultural capacities to revise would inevitably atrophy.

Despite some notable exceptions today, it appears that not enough curriculums nationwide are designed to foster capabilities prerequisite for exercising the nation's dissent-oriented constitutional rights. Seldom do we ask ourselves, for example, what it would mean to equip the young so that they could better exercise their right to "petition the government for a redress of grievance." Seldom do we ask what it would mean to think through, with students, possible interpretations of the Declaration's "right to alter and abolish" clause. Why shouldn't whole classrooms, for instance, contemplate what legal and cultural forms deserve to be altered or abolished, or what novel legal and cultural forms should be invented by acts of political creativity given our present-day needs? As we read in Chapter 2, the dissent-oriented rights were established in order to keep the government aligned with its official or putative purpose of promoting human rights and the general welfare of the American people. In fully recognizing the value of dissent for our survival as a republic, it seems obvious that this value and principle must become a foundational cornerstone of the emerging civic education curriculum.

The objective to educate the young so that they will become conversant with dissent-oriented rights, values, and actions, immediately raises the question of how the term *dissent* might be defined. Not all forms of dissent, certainly, are non-violent; yet democratic forms of dissent are non-violent. In recognizing the almost endless variations, gradations, and emotional intensities of dissent, how to distinguish between its healthy and unhealthy forms? The philosopher of education Sarah Stitzlein, in her valuable book, *Teaching for Dissent*, offers a comprehensive and multifaceted response to this and other tricky moral quandaries that invariably arise when teachers privilege dissent. She remarks:

Employing democratic dissent is a way of living with each other that is open to change and critique, and is also a way of questioning governance and keeping it accountable to members of a state. The role and appreciation of dissent as fundamental to a vibrant democracy has varied in America since its inception.[1]

Stitzlein effectively captures the crucial linkage between dissent and receptivity to critical thought and social change. In observing that the "appreciation of dissent" has "varied in America since its inception," Stitzlein perhaps formulates this point too gently. It may be more accurate to say that appreciation of dissent in America, especially in light of its revolutionary heritage, has been revoltingly underappreciated throughout the nation's political and educational history.[2]

Be that as it may, Stitzlein correctly argues that teachers who wish to highlight the value of dissent in their classrooms need to find ways to defuse the concerns of those who may be inclined to think that "teaching for dissent" functions merely as a fig leaf for covering up what is essentially anti-American propaganda. As a counterpoise to this type of criticism, Stitzlein wisely invites teachers to focus as much attention on reconstructive remedies to social problems as they do on deconstructive forms of critique. In striking an admirable Jeffersonian revisionary balance, Stitzlein writes that, "good dissenters use creativity and imagination to envision and construct improved alternatives that move a community out of a negative past and into a positive future."[3]

It seems that students would sooner begin to appreciate dissent as a wholesome American value and activity, if they had a better sense that every *democratic* achievement in US history—the abolition of slavery, the abolition of child labor, women's suffrage, the legalization of unions, the

---

[1] Sarah Stitzlein, *Teaching for Dissent: Citizenship Education and Political Activism*. New York: Routledge, 2013, 69.

[2] For example, as a barometer of America's frequently ambivalent attitude toward dissent, examine the so-called Colin Kaepernick controversy. Whereby this noted NFL player was banished from the league for "taking a knee" during the playing of the National Anthem to protest patterns of police brutality. Kaepernick and other players were severely berated apparently for desanctifying two important religious rituals in American culture: football and the Star Spangled Banner. After having been "blackballed" from the NFL for his peaceful dissent, Kaepernick sued the NFL, and a civil court in California recently awarded him an undisclosed monetary sum.

[3] Stitzlein, 69.

legalization of same-sex marriage, to name a few—came about as a result of brave dissenters who championed unpopular causes. It is no exaggeration to say, then, that any official repression of teaching for dissent can only have a deteriorating effect on efforts to renew civic education on a Jeffersonian basis.

Although the activity of dissent has been theoretically separated from the capacity to revise in this chapter for purposes of clarification, ultimately the two categories are deeply entwined. Metaphorically speaking, "dissent" and "revision" are two sides of the same coin. Or, stated with slightly more precision, dissent implies the *ethical willingness to act to revise*, while the capacity to revise, refers to a prior human *ontological possibility*. At the center of Jefferson's revolutionary theory, there is an implicit recognition of the need for republican regimes to bring both human capabilities into mature fruition: revision, as a human and psychological capacity for transformation, and dissent, as an ethical and political capacity for civic action.

Rechanneling the Mythopoetic Spirit of 76

The case has been made in several chapters that the moral and political foundations of Jefferson's revolutionary theory are connected to his conception of the Spirit of 76, understood here as a rhetorical trope and symbolic container of specific democratic moral values and philosophic principles. Importantly, in Onuf and Reed's magisterial book on Jefferson, the Spirit of 76 is indexed 10 times.[4] A review of these and other references reveals that Jefferson used this discourse, or rhetoric, to corral into one phrase all of the deeper, "exceptional" qualities and meanings he attributed to a democratic conception of American identity. Jefferson usually invokes the phrase in a kind of jeremiadic fashion. He does this by citing the possibilities for future progress that could accrue from allegiance to its underlying principles. But Jefferson also laments that the spirit's moral resonance and power was at risk (in his own day) of being forgotten by the American public, a prospect tantamount to the end of the revolution as Jefferson knew it. Any forgetting of the Spirit of 76, then

---

[4] Annette Gordon-Reed and Peter Onuf, *"Most Blessed of the Patriarchs" Thomas Jefferson and the Empire of Imagination*. New York: W. W. Norton & Company, 2016, 368.

or now, would inevitably be accompanied by a forgetting of the Declaration itself, as this document forms the existential guts of that spirit. How, then, to recover the value of the Declaration? Is it salvageable?

Instead of interpreting the text of the Declaration exclusively as a product of either Jefferson's hand or of the few editors who helped craft its final version, we ought to regard it, as Jefferson did, as a historical snapshot of an established common sense of the American people.[5] The distinction is crucial: it indicates that Jefferson wasn't wildly "out front" of the American people in authoring the document, as much as he was acting as a scribe reflecting the common sense of the American people. Writing in 1825 to Henry Lee, Jefferson takes no personal credit for its insights:

> Neither aiming at originality of principle or sentiment, nor yet copied from any particular previous writing, it was intended to be an expression of the American mind, and to give to that expression the proper tone and spirit called for by the occasion. All its authority rests on the harmonizing sentiments of the day, whether expressed in conversation, in letters, or in the elementary books of public right, as [is found in] Aristotle, Cicero, Locke, Sidney, &c.[6]

Let's pause for a moment and consider the implications that Jefferson's statement has for the broader purposes of this inquiry. In many chapters, we have been talking a lot about "recovering" the Spirit of 76 as a basis for recovering both the civic purposes of American education and, more broadly, the democratic potential of the American experiment. What needs stressing here is that which is being recovered is not the insights of any individual. Rather, what we're ultimately talking about is a recovery of a national form of common sense that, at one point, appeared to command the legitimate consent of the people.

It is difficult of course to gauge the level of consensus there may or may not have been in the 1770s regarding the status of the enlightenment-inspired human rights and democratic principles reflected in the Declaration of Independence. Nonetheless, the release of the document had the practical effect of making ideological conflicts over the meaning of its

---

[5] This argument is found in Pauline Maier's, *American Scripture: Making the Declaration of Independence* (1997), and more recently, in Danielle Allen's, *Our Declaration: A Reading of the Declaration of Independence in Defense of Equality* (2014).

[6] Thomas Jefferson to Richard Henry Lee, May 8, 1825.

defining principles, such as equality, the vital starting point for ongoing negotiations of national identity. Indeed, Jefferson's revolutionary theory is premised on the need to cultivate the ability of the American people to participate with these tensions—to live the questions—so that it might serve regenerative purposes, as Americans rediscovered the meaning of its core principles in ever-changing historical contexts. His revolutionary theory falls to pieces however if the memory of that which defines the Spirit of 76 is somehow forgotten, or otherwise dissolves into the ether.

In previous chapters, we've seen that Dewey, Counts, and Allen similarly recognized that amnesia with respect to the nation's first principles would signal the end of the revolutionary project of democratic transition. They share the conviction that the principles of the Declaration, if they are to become meaningful, cannot simply be memorized in a hollow mechanical sense, but studied and actively interpreted in light of present-day problems and needs. If we assume, as we probably should, that the symbolic currency of the Spirit of 76 now exists in a state of virtual free fall, it's imperative to explore how this admittedly elusive signifier might be reframed with greater conceptual precision in order to facilitate its imaginative recovery.

The Apple of Gold and the Picture of Silver: How Lincoln's Fragment on the Constitution and Union Extends Jefferson's Rhetoric of the Spirit of 76

A more robustly democratic, civic-purposed classroom must initiate students into the project of reframing—probably for the first time—the rather complicated, but pedagogically fecund, relationship between the Declaration and the Constitution. Few historical figures write about the dynamics of this relationship as cogently, as philosophically, as aesthetically, or indeed, as tragically as Abraham Lincoln in his "Fragment on the Constitution and Union."[7] To connect our discussion of Lincoln's fragment to the book's larger purposes, we can situate the text as a glowing piece of democratic rhetoric, one that beautifully mirrors Jefferson's attempts to name the Spirit of 76.

---

[7] *The Collected Works of Abraham Lincoln*, Vol. 4, ed. Roy Basler. New Brunswick: Rutgers University Press, 1953, 167–168.

The poetic imagery and analytical distinctions that Lincoln introduces to clarify the complicated interface between the Declaration and the Constitution, amplify, in instructive ways, the core features of Jefferson's revolutionary theory of democratic transition. The fragment also offers an attractive, philosophically based representation of what Jefferson called the Spirit of 76. Lincoln invents two key tropes, the Apple of Gold and Picture of Silver, as a means for defining the Spirit of 76 as well as to identify the critical moral hierarchy that exists between the Declaration and Constitution.

Lincoln composes his fragment on the precipice of the Civil War, in January 1861, no doubt with great trepidation about the survival of the republic. In writing it, Lincoln appears guided by a desire to lend intelligibility to the little understood yet significant differences between the Declaration and Constitution. In doing so, Lincoln offers a compelling democratic image of American identity, an aspirational moral image that, tellingly, is said to have an underlying "philosophical cause."[8] Lincoln insists, like Jefferson before him, that the nation is rooted in a moral proposition which runs deeper, he says, than either the desire for independence, for material acquisition, or for a mere change of masters. Lincoln muses that this idea consisted of something

> ...entwining itself more closely about the human heart than even our great prosperity. It is the principle of liberty to all—the principle that clears the path for all—gives hope to all—and by consequence, enterprise and industry to all.[9]

Lincoln's repetition of the phrase, "to all," as a qualifying condition to establish the moral legitimacy of liberty, hope, enterprise, and industry, indicates that he is invoking the principle of equality as a core value of American identity. Both the imagery and analysis that Lincoln deploys to capture the idea of America's democratic moral identity, similarly reflects Jefferson's various representations of the Spirit of 76 as a spiritual essence anchored in a philosophical idea.

Lincoln first identifies the vital *interactive* relation between the two charters and thereby provides a theoretical scaffolding for interpreting the perpetually unfinished character of American democracy. Broadly

[8] Ibid., 167.
[9] Ibid., 168.

construed, Lincoln's framing of the interactivity between the two charters describes the moral and political tensions that arise when a set of
moral/human rights—symbolized by the Declaration—exist alongside a
set of legal/property rights—symbolized by the Constitution.[10]
   Inquiry into the fluid zone of tensions that emerge from this epic and
ongoing clash between the nation's democratic moral aspirations, on the
one hand, and its existing legal structures on the other, can reveal a great
deal about the frequently perplexing trajectories of American political and
educational history.
   Building on Danielle Allen's trailblazing pedagogical treatment of the
Declaration,[11] we have a solid foundation for treating the moral and legal
tensions that define the interface between the nation's two birth certificates as the new ground zero for civic educators. If such a focus were
regarded as one of the central intellectual labors of democratic-minded
teachers, it would encourage students—now as civic cartographers of
America's moral geography—to awaken to the perils, the possibilities, and
the ethical predicaments of being democratic and living in a viable democratic culture.
   To return to the text of the fragment, after making these crucial preliminary analytical distinctions, Lincoln, as noted, proceeds to furnish readers with a tremendously important political and moral judgement. He
informs his fellow Americans that the philosophical principle which the
Declaration embodies,

   ...has proven to be an "apple of gold" to us. The Union and the Constitution, are the "picture of silver," subsequently framed around it.[12]

If the "apple" can be taken to symbolize knowledge, and "gold" symbolizes the highest form of that knowledge, then the apple of gold is
deployed as a core signifier of a moral democratic essence. It is quite
extraordinary here that Lincoln elevates the moral and democratic values

---

[10]This interpretive approach was championed by Jefferson, but also by other notable
figures in American intellectual history, from Charles Beard and Vernon Parrington to
Merrill Peterson and Garry Wills.

[11]As has been emphasized throughout the book, Danielle Allen's, *Our Declaration*
should be required reading for civic educators interested in making the Declaration and
the principle of equality central themes of their pedagogy.

[12]Lincoln, 168.

of the Declaration above the Constitution, which he clearly codes as a subordinate legal instrument. In associating the *moral/human rights* Declaration with *gold,* and the *legal/property rights* Constitution with *silver,* Lincoln expresses his belief that the moral principles of the Declaration must be valued over and above its legal structures. In Lincoln's words:

> The picture was made, not to conceal or destroy the apple, but to adorn and preserve it. The picture was made for the apple—not the apple for the picture.[13]

In declaring that the picture was made for the apple—not the apple for the picture—Lincoln deems the substantive moral, philosophical, and human rights purposes of the Declaration paramount. The great truth that Lincoln, and Jefferson before him, both articulate and what we need to remember today, is that the values of the Declaration (human rights) must form the basis of America's democratic identity, and that the sole purpose of an amendable Constitution is to protect and extend those purposes.[14]

With the specter of Civil War imminent, Lincoln knows the apple's very existence is placed in existential jeopardy (not unlike today). Lincoln implies that the legalization of slavery written into the picture of silver, had caused the nation's legal structure to exist in direct contradiction to the moral and philosophical premises upon which American identity, symbolized by the apple of gold, was founded. With the crisis at hand, Lincoln sounds a jeremiadic warning:

> So let us act, that neither picture or apple shall ever be blurred, or bruised or broken. That we may so act, we must study, and understand the points of danger.[15]

Here Lincoln acknowledges a frightening, tragic possibility: That the magnificent, philosophically grounded, human rights qualities of the

---

[13] Ibid, 168.

[14] Yet, across the nation, millions of eighth graders will engage in a mechanized ritual called a Constitution test, while our education and curriculum leaders ignore the far more crucial and potentially empowering moral foundations of the Declaration—an omission that is anything but "politically neutral." Chapter 10 elaborates further on this problem under the rubric of "Civic Philosophy."

[15] Lincoln, 168.

apple of gold as well as its legal instrument, the picture of silver, could, in fact, be potentially destroyed. Lincoln seems to be saying that Americans need to awaken to the moral supremacy of the Declaration, and need also to pay attention to the power-laden interplay of forces—moral, economic, and political—that may corrupt the two primary channeling devices of American political culture.

Finally, Lincoln's brief jeremiad affirms Jefferson's earlier forecast that the survival of the republic would depend on a national commitment to expanding realms of public intelligence. Notice, for example, how seamlessly Lincoln connects our ability to act directly to our ability to study… "that we may so act, we must study, and understand the points of danger." In making these connections, Lincoln aptly synthesizes the heart of Jefferson's educational and revolutionary theory. For in the absence of a popular awareness of the points of danger, i.e., without an alert and engaged citizenry that can identify danger points, the values and principles sequestered within the apple of gold would surely become bruised, broken, or forgotten. A critical remembering of the Declaration, then, including its associated rhetoric, such as can be found in the Spirit of 76 and Apple of Gold, can and should serve as a foundational template for redirecting the purposes of civic education. On what other basis but the Declaration can Americans be guided toward a democratic future?

CHAPTER 10

Reimagining Educational Purpose Through Jeffersonian Categories

This chapter presents a necessary preliminary conceptual justification for the curricular renovations proposed in our final chapter. To frame this chapter's general direction and lend substance to arguments developed in Chapter 11, three of Jefferson's most radical moral propositions—*the earth belongs to the living*, the *pursuit of happiness*, and the *alter and abolish* clause—shall form its conceptual foundation.

Why rely on these Jeffersonian categories as a conceptual foundation for our proposed curricular renovations? Simply put, taken together, they will serve as springboards for catapulting Jefferson's revolutionary theory into the here and now. As critical moral propositions, they offer a powerful justification for the need to reconstruct educational purposes today. As noted in previous chapters, *the earth belongs to the living* emerges as a vital Jeffersonian heuristic for this inquiry because, in effect, it boldly proclaims to every present-day American generation: Do not permit demonstrably obsolete ideas and practices of the past to govern your life. Do not permit the inherited values, thought patterns, and presumed wisdom of the past to be morally binding if they no longer serve your generation's existing and developing needs as you define them.

As separate yet related revolutionary principles, the *pursuit of happiness* and *alter and abolish* clauses can be interpreted as related to *the earth belongs to the living*, in that their potential meanings are similarly generationally dependent. That is, the meanings of these phrases should not be interpreted as pre-established and static. More productively, they can

© The Author(s) 2020   155
K. T. Burch, *Jefferson's Revolutionary Theory and the Reconstruction of Educational Purpose*, The Cultural and Social Foundations of Education, https://doi.org/10.1007/978-3-030-45763-1_10

attain fresh meaning only through generational interpretation and rein-terpretation. For the *pursuit of happiness* and *alter and abolish* clauses, similar to *the earth belongs to the living*, boldly proclaim to every present-day American generation: Judge for yourselves the state of your political world; judge for yourselves whether existing governmental and cultural forms and purposes are likely—or not—to promote your own sense of safety and happiness.

Taken in their ideal, embodied forms, all three pieces of political rhetoric involve citizens making political judgments and moral distinc-tions regarding the quality of their personal and social realities. As we saw in earlier chapters, here I am echoing Danielle Allen's articulation that the Declaration reflects a "beautiful optimism" that ordinary people are capable of judging whether or not they are happy with existing politi-cal, social or, in our case, educational forms and arrangements. Accord-ing to Allen, these types of judgment reflect a form of political equal-ity that we all share: "This is what is so dazzling in the Declaration: its unbounded optimism in the capacity of human beings to see the future in the present well enough—not perfectly, but well enough—to move toward securing happiness. Thanks to this capacity, we are collectively able 'to alter or abolish' our existing government and to institute new Govern-ment, laying its foundation on such principles and organizing its powers in such form, as to [us] shall seem most likely to effect [our] Safety and Happiness."[1]

In considering how the *alter and abolish* clause might be applied to our present historical moment, let's recall that Sheldon Wolin's broad inter-pretation of the clause, discussed in Chapter 2, stipulated that it should be understood to refer not only to a change in governmental forms but also to a change in *cultural forms*.[2] The analytical distinction is significant. It broadens considerably the scope of potential political creativity to include non-state-oriented civic commitments and actions taken in the realm of civil society.[3] In our present context, then, the claim here is not that we

---

[1] Danielle Allen, "Beautiful Optimism." In *Our Declaration: A Reading of the Declara-tion of Independence in Defense of Equality*. New York: W. W. Norton, 2014, 186.

[2] See Page 15 in Chapter 2 for a fuller discussion of this theme. Sheldon Wolin, "What Revolutionary Action Means Today." In *Dimensions of Radical Democracy: Pluralism, Citizenship, Community*, ed. Chantal Mouffe. London: Verso, 1992.

[3] The term civil society, for our purposes, can be defined broadly as that sphere which organizes itself outside the boundaries of both the state and the economic spheres. The

should abolish the state itself in the form of the US government. Rather, I am proposing that Americans today need to think seriously about altering and abolishing certain educational forms and their corresponding curricular purposes which governments sponsor at the state and federal level, and replace them with new educational forms and purposes, so as to better effect our safety and happiness.

In addition, the curricular renovations outlined in Chapter 11 also represent an homage to Jefferson's well-known penchant for engaging in curricular experimentation. This spirit of curricular experimentation is perhaps symbolized most prominently by the establishment of the University of Virginia, 1824–1825 (henceforth, *UVA*). It undoubtedly signifies one of his finest legacies. For our purposes, UVA's creative invention can be interpreted as one of several conceptual pillars of Jefferson's revolutionary theory. As we have seen, most of his attempts at educational and curricular innovation failed, at least legislatively. Yet, toward the end of his life, Jefferson worked hard to bring about the establishment of the *UVA*. The complicated story of how Jefferson and his educational allies brought about this magnificent achievement lies beyond the scope of our inquiry.[4] However, a few reflections on the subject may help clarify the revolutionary character of Jefferson's experimental institution-creation. Perhaps the most decisive consequence of this innovation was that it signaled the beginning of the end of the church's centuries-long monopoly of power over institutions of higher education in the United States.[5]

To further concretize the revolutionary character of Jefferson's creative institution-making, we turn to the Rockfish Gap Report (1818),

---

realm of civil society in the United States has been praised by no less a figure than Alexis de Tocqueville as constituting the truly democratic zone of American political culture. All of the social movements that have democratized the country, for example, began first within the sphere of civil society. For an excellent genealogical analysis of civil society within the Western tradition, including the United States, see John Ehrenberg, "Civil Society and Democratic Politics." In *Civil Society: The Critical History of an Idea*. New York: New York University Press, 1999, 233–250.

[4] A noted Jefferson specialist has recently published an exceedingly fine-grained history of the origins of UVA, one that highlights not only Jefferson's "limited" educational visions during his final years, but also his use of slave labor in the building of UVA. See Alan Taylor, *Thomas Jefferson's Education*. New York: W. W. Norton, 2019.

[5] Cameron Addis, "Christian Opposition to UVA." In *Jefferson's Vision for Education, 1760–1845*. New York: Peter Lang, 2003, 68–87.

a document he authored, which represented the ideological and curricular blueprint for the new university.[6] Shockingly for many, Jefferson's blueprint included neither a department of religion or even a single professor of religion.[7] This effort by Jefferson to "reconstitute" educational purpose, of course, represented a radical break from centuries of curricular precedent.

In a larger sense, acting as an agent of the enlightenment, Jefferson dethroned religious faith as an underlying value and purpose of the university, and elevated in its place the new secular god of reason. The university's purposes would now be secular and civic, just as the purposes of the free public schools that Jefferson envisioned were to be secular and civic. The secularization of both primary and higher education marked the end of the church's hegemony over the field of education in the United States. Yet, it also heralded the beginning of another tradition—that of American universities conceiving of their mission in terms of serving a common good, rather than in terms of serving congregants in this or that religious sect. And while historians tell us that the secular and civic-purposed founding of *UVA* produced a backlash against Jefferson's reputation in Virginia at the time—reviving old canards about his alleged atheism—few would dare suggest today that *UVA* or other public universities should change their secular identity and mission.

Thus, considered as an early eighteenth-century model of curricular innovation, the *UVA* example ought to qualify as revolutionary both for its immediate and long-term effects.[8] This is particularly so when we recognize how audaciously Jefferson dispensed with centuries of entrenched educational practice. Perhaps because of his expertise in so many fields of scientific and artistic endeavor, Jefferson quite readily articulated the formation of new branches of learning, new categories of inquiry, and crucially, new civic values and purposes for the university to fulfill. In describing Jefferson's zeal for inventing new curricular structures and traditions, historian Cameron Addis observes that, "in the Enlightenment

[6] Thomas Jefferson's Draft of the Rockfish Gap Report of the University of Virginia Commissioners. June 28, 1818. https://founders.archives.gov/documents/Jefferson/03-13-02-0197-0004.

[7] David Tyack, "Forming the National Character: Paradox in the Educational Thought of the Revolutionary Generation." *Harvard Educational Review*, Vol. 36, 1966, 29–40.

[8] Jennings L. Wagoner, Jr. "Jefferson's Educational Legacy." In *Jefferson and Education*. Chapel Hill: University of North Carolina Press, 127–146.

tradition, Jefferson loved to tinker with categories."[9] Given the historically entrenched educational forms that he inherited and was attempting to transcend, Jefferson was required to "tinker with categories"—and in consequential ways.

TINKERING WITH NEW CATEGORIES (OF MEANING), CA. 2020

Considering our purposes, we cannot help but ask how Jefferson's curricular creativity and innovation might serve today as a kind of moral beacon for guiding needed renovations of curricular organization and purpose. As we've seen, at the root of Jefferson's revolutionary theory, resides the recognition that, as historical conditions change and as human needs change, individuals and institutions must change to keep pace with the times. As I have argued, once we appreciate the ways in which this Jeffersonian principle of *inevitable change* undergirds the moral ideals of *the earth belongs to the living*, the *pursuit of happiness* and the *alter and abolish* clauses, the potential meaning of each phrase is revealed at their deeper levels. Broadly put, the principle of change and the need for civic agents and institutions to respond intelligently to that change is what gives our three phrase's their fundamental temporal and intergenerational social character. In other words, the psychic guts of Jefferson's revolutionary theory—that which ultimately enables its empirical expression—is the human capacity to revise itself in the context of changing circumstances and needs.

The Jeffersonian perception of ceaseless change must inform our deeper interpretations of each of these sublime pieces of democratic rhetoric. They ought to be interpreted by educators not only as interesting pieces of rhetoric, but preeminently as instruments of political questioning—instruments whose underlying spirit of radical democratic scrutiny can be recruited pedagogically to interrogate existing ideas and institutions. Ultimately, then, regardless of the label we attach to these Jeffersonian categories (e.g., moral ideals, categories of meaning, pieces of democratic rhetoric, instruments of political questioning, or pillars of his revolutionary theory) they should never be interpreted as inert, objectively existent, prefixed essences. Rather, their fluid, provisional meanings

---

[9] Addis, 186.

may come to life via interpretation only in persons living in the present—persons who the Declaration empowers to make judgments about their inherited world, and judgments about their happiness, and whether their governments—or school systems—are adequately promoting the human rights-oriented needs of the current generation.[10]

With this conceptual framing in mind, then, let us take inspiration from Jefferson's spirit of educational experimentation and engage in some necessary tinkering with categories. Before commencing with the next sequence of this thought experiment, however, it's worth repeating that the chief aim in tinkering with new categories of the curricular organization is not merely to rearrange the chairs on a sinking Titanic. Instead, to continue the maritime metaphor, the point is to inspire the passengers of the ship—We the People—to take control of its helm so as to change the ship's direction. More specifically, the intention is to smooth the path, conceptually, for the schools to embody fundamentally new purposes—purposes that would jettison the values and purposes that now guide the corporate-driven neoliberal paradigm of education. The chapter is thus offered as a stimulus to readers, inviting them to exercise their moral and political imaginations as they think through the contradictions, the limits, and the future possibilities of American public education.

Similar to the intended function of the Rockfish Gap Report, I want to propose new branches of inquiry and relocate existing disciplines under alternative curricular headings. The primary educational institution, or practice, earmarked for abolition within this realignment would be the use of high-stakes testing as the central organizing principle of education. As noted, one of the hoped-for outcomes of these curricular reforms is to help bring today's public school curriculum much closer to actually meeting the needs of the next generation of Americans. One key claim here is the belief that the neoliberal paradigm of education has failed most egregiously in its responsibility to promote the democratic civic purposes of education—and this factor alone ought to prove fatal to its moral legitimacy. More Americans must learn to see that the defining tenets of

---

[10] As we saw in Chapter 2, Jefferson defined a generation based on twenty-year intervals. The generation born on or around 2000, for example, might be dubbed the "9/11 generation" to denote their coming of age in the shadow of permanent war, and thus also the generation that has been most ensnared in its fatal domestic consequences, from a culture of high-stakes testing and student debt to a culture of celebrity and ecological collapse.

neoliberal education make it nearly impossible for it to respond, in any meaningful sense, to the authentic needs of American youth.

Surely, as democratic citizens, we appreciate that the claim of identifying any given generation's "authentic needs" is necessarily a debatable proposition. As Jefferson's three revolutionary propositions imply, however, owing to the unrelenting march of Time itself, the project of identifying the authentic as opposed to the false needs of any given generation, can never be answered definitively for all time. New human needs will always be historically emergent. What follows in Chapter 11, then, reflects no pretense of having developed a set of tidy remedies for what ails public education today. It is instead a provocation for readers to think anew, through Jeffersonian categories, about the genuine needs of America's youth and about the future of American public education. The curricular renovations presented below in capsule form and discussed more fully in the following chapter, may well disappoint some readers. The discussions in Chapter 11, for example, do not include explanations for how these curricular renovations might be institutionally implemented or how they might be further unpacked conceptually. Those aspects of my proposals, as crucial as they may be, lie beyond the scope of the book. After all, the singular beauty of thought experiments is that, in conducting them, we can avoid being thrown into imaginative inaction by mundane logistical considerations. Upon closer examination, frankly, these types of considerations often reduce to *inherited* forms of common sense that whisper in our ears that which we cannot do. Instead, our gold standard is to ask: What is the right thing to do? What ought to happen? In this manner, then, each of the three sections of Chapter 11 is intended to present limited "snapshots" of new moral directions in curricular renovation, glimpses of what ought to happen in relation to reconstructing educational purpose.

Given these analytical distinctions and caveats, I propose that the actual educational needs of the next generation of Americans can be generalized into three separable yet related categories, each of which corresponds to three separable yet related curricular branches of learning:

- The need to recover civic selfhood
- The need for ecological literacy
- The need to value matters of fact and truth in a media-saturated environment.

In our next chapter, I contend that the three interrelated needs identified above eclipse in relevance the dreary register of student needs that now dominate the neoliberal paradigm of education. Within the logic of its curriculum, for example, we see manifest an apparent *need* to valorize high-stakes testing; an apparent *need* to cut and delegitimize the civics, the arts, and the humanities. Nor does this curricular pattern operate in isolation, for it also exists in relation to an apparent *need* to monetize schools as lucrative new zones of profit making. In other words, corporate-defined needs monopolize the construction of educational purposes today. As an imagined counterpoise to the neoliberal paradigm of education, our final chapter is an attempt to reconstruct educational purposes according to a Jeffersonian vision of educational needs and values.

CHAPTER 11

Jeffersonian Directions in Curricular Renovation

The first sequence of our thought experiment begins by suggesting the kind of necessary constitutional and economic changes within the political economy of the United States that would be required to support financially our new proposals for curricular renovation. The second sequence outlines, via a one-page diagram, the broad contours of what I am calling the K-12 Curricular Redesign. The third and lengthier sequence articulates, from a Jeffersonian perspective, a set of arguments to establish a solid moral foundation for each of the new categories of curricular renovation.

THE POLITICAL ECONOMY OF REVIVING A JEFFERSONIAN CIVIC-PURPOSED K-12 EDUCATION FOR ALL

Let us recall from Chapter 8 that in Jefferson's 1806 State of the Union address, the president called for a new amendment to the US Constitution in order to validate and protect a public establishment of education. His rationale for constitutionalizing education stemmed, in large part, from the belief that such an amendment, as he imagined it, would ensure that the institution's financial footing would operate as independently as possible from expenditures on the military establishment. Jefferson's discussion of this aspect of the amendment is critical. Among other things, it reminds us that the formula for funding public education that Jefferson envisioned is a vital component of the amendment proposal. Jefferson

K. T. Burch, *Jefferson's Revolutionary Theory and the Reconstruction of Educational Purpose*, The Cultural and Social Foundations of Education, https://doi.org/10.1007/978-3-030-45763-1_11

shrewdly anticipated that resources earmarked for education would tend always to be diverted to the military, in his words, "whenever a speck of war was on the horizon."[1] Similarly, we observed in previous chapters that President Eisenhower identified the same morally problematic relation between educational and military expenditures in the twentieth century. For when Ike declared that the nation's military expenditures prevented needed school buildings from being built, he provides a vivid illustration of how inordinate levels of military spending, always *subtracts* resources from domestic institutions that could contribute so much to expanding the quality of American democracy.

Therefore, as we look to apply Jefferson's revolutionary theory to the contemporary educational scene for the purpose of reconstructing its moral purposes, it is reasonable to assert the following. (1) A right to a civic-purposed public education should be protected under the US Constitution and, (2) a substantial source of funding for the public schools could be derived from redirecting 10% of the $800 billion dollars annual war budget for use in the Department of Education. In 2020 terms, this would add $80 billion to the proposed FY 2020 federal education budget of $59.9 billion which would more than double current spending, a financial boon that could be utilized to implement the full potential of the new constitutional decree.[2]

Also contained in Jefferson's (1806) State of the Union address was the idea that federal lands should be relied upon to establish an enduring basis for funding a public establishment of education. Perhaps today the moral spirit behind this Jeffersonian formula for funding public education can be recovered and employed as a heuristic to inspire novel remedies for solving the problem of public school inequality. To clarify, for example, most Americans would be shocked to learn of the magnitude of the military's domestic and global landholdings.[3] Thus, a contemporary

[1] For more on this discussion, see Chapter 8.

[2] See Impact of the President's FY 2020 Budget on K-12 Education. firstfocus.org/wp-content/uploads/2019/04/FACT-SHEET-Presidents-FY20-Budget-K-12-Education.pdf.

[3] For this information, I have relied on three sources, as follows:

   a. The Department of Defense Base Structure Report, Fiscal Year 2018 Baseline: A Summary of the Real Property Inventory Data. Acq.osd.mil/eie/downloads/BSI/Base%20%Structure%20Report%FY18.pdf.
   b. How Much Land Military Bases Take Up in Each State. http://www.businessinsider.com/how-much-land-military-bases-take-up-in-each-state.

Jeffersonian approach would examine the tremendous dollar value of the assets embodied in the military's vast landholdings. Notably, these assets would include the military's many ocean-side bases and spectacular, luxury golf courses—located in Hawai'i and around the globe. As part of the educational reform agenda going forward, at least from a Jeffersonian standpoint, we increasingly need to ask policymakers: Why shouldn't these untapped resources be explored as a viable means for providing public education with an enduring economic foundation?

In thinking through the problem of funding a civic-purposed public education—one that would also work to ameliorate the system's structural inequalities—we would do well to remind ourselves that Jefferson was adamant that the national security of the United States was directly linked to its ability to develop the intelligence of its people. Jefferson considered the intelligence and virtue of the American people the best available "weapon," as it were, for protecting against threats to its republican existence. Now more than ever, it seems clear we need to recover this Jeffersonian precept.

One additional advantage of constitutionalizing a right to a civic-purposed education would be that the value of both civic education and the humanities would certainly rebound from their present moribund state. As Stephen Lurie's article in the *Atlantic Monthly* aptly describes, every nation that has adopted a legal and national right to education has also developed a demonstrably more robust "educational culture" as a result. Americans need constant reminding that while the United States is the wealthiest nation in the world, our global educational ranking of 17th can only be regarded as mediocre. Revealingly, Lurie writes, "every country that outperforms the U.S. has a constitutional or statutory commitment to this right." Lurie sums up what would likely result from such a legal and moral renovation:

> If a true right is established, soft forces and hard law can begin to fundamentally alter the immense flaws of the education system nationwide. This is the exact phenomenon that plays out time and again in other countries— and particularly the ones besting American education. The constitutional guarantee develops a national culture of education, a baseline for rights,

---

c. David Vine, *Base Nation: How U.S. Military Bases Abroad Harm America and the World*. New York: Metropolitan Books, 2015.

and allows—if necessary—the legal protection of that standard. Such an amendment won't be a panacea for American education, but without it the U.S. will stay average in the rankings and yet remain that one country left behind.[4]

Skeptics of this proposal may understandably argue that Jefferson would be the last person to embrace such an expansion of federal power. More pointedly, they may ask:

> Would Jefferson—who was committed to local determination and control of the schools—want the federal government to impose a particular form of public education on states and communities?

Let us address the apparent contradiction the question highlights. At first glance, Jefferson's reputation as a "strict" constitutional construc-tionist would seem to preclude his support for constitutionalizing a fed-eral right to education. As a strict constructionist, Jefferson did not want to grant any powers to the federal government unless there was some urgent need to do so. However, a review of the historical record sug-gests that Jefferson's strict constructionist view of federal power should be taken almost with a grain of salt, or at least, with several profound caveats. We find below several important instances that flatly contradict Jefferson's limited/strict construction of federal power:

- The Louisiana Purchase (1803), where Jefferson offers up a stunning repudiation of his strict constructionism.
- The constitutional proposal (1787) for the federal government to intervene in the private economy to restrict corporate monopolies.
- The constitutional proposal (1787) for the federal government to intervene to suppress the development of a war-industry, i.e., to pro-hibit standing armies.
- The constitutional proposal (1806) for the federal government to establish and protect some form of public education.
- The Embargo Acts (1807–1808), an assertion of federal power over states and localities to shut down their trans-Atlantic commerce (in order to avoid a war).

---

[4] Steven Lurie, "Why Doesn't the Constitution Guarantee a Right to Education." *The Atlantic*, October 16, 2013.

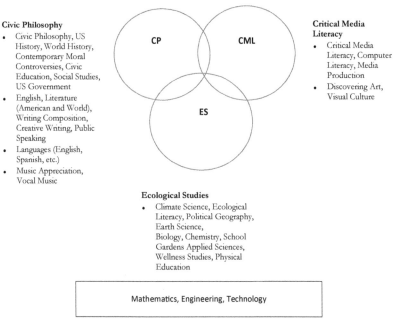

Civic Philosophy
- Civic Philosophy, US History, World History, Contemporary Moral Controversies, Civic Education, Social Studies, US Government
- English, Literature (American and World), Writing Composition, Creative Writing, Public Speaking
- Languages (English, Spanish, etc.)
- Music Appreciation, Vocal Music

Critical Media Literacy
- Critical Media Literacy, Computer Literacy, Media Production
- Discovering Art, Visual Culture

Ecological Studies
- Climate Science, Ecological Literacy, Political Geography, Earth Science, Biology, Chemistry, School Gardens Applied Sciences, Wellness Studies, Physical Education

Mathematics, Engineering, Technology

Fig. 11.1 The K-12 curricular redesign

The larger point suggested here is that if circumstances demanded it—as Jefferson interpreted those circumstances—he was quite capable of taking positions that would extend federal power, particularly when he thought that the nation's survival was at stake.

I believe it is warranted to assert, once again, that Jefferson would be revolted at the erosion of public education today, especially given its "neo-colonial" character. If current trajectories are not strongly resisted, we shall soon witness the death of public education as we know it. For this reason, it seems warranted to assert that Jefferson would recognize the need to bring a civic-purposed K-12 public education under the protection of the federal constitution. Finally, I refer readers to what Peter Onuf, the noted Jefferson specialist, wrote about Jefferson's attitude toward the use of federal power: "Spending on education constituted the grand and significant exception to Jefferson's minimal state."[5] (Fig. 11.1).

[5] Onuf, as cited in Jennings L. Wagoner, Jr., "Jefferson's Educational Legacy." Thomas Jefferson Foundation, Monticello Monograph Series. Chapel Hill: University of North Carolina Press, 2004, 129–130.

CIVIC PHILOSOPHY (THE NEED
FOR DEMOCRATIC SELFHOOD)

As previous chapters have suggested, Jefferson would no doubt be appalled today at those nationwide curricular policies that have radically diminished the value of the civics and humanities. He understood that these traditions form the basis of a democratic society. He would no doubt regard today's neoliberal "reforms" as symbols of a resurgent anti-enlightenment tendency within American political culture. As Jefferson rolls in his grave, we can almost hear him pleading with us today... *where's the emphasis on critical thinking, on reason, on exercising the moral sense, and on learning about the ideological mechanisms that pose threats to our fragile experiment in self-government?*

As a creative response to these fictive, yet well-grounded Jeffersonian queries, let the following proposal be submitted to the teachers of the nation, to policymakers, and to concerned citizens. Henceforth, all existing social studies, government, history, literature, writing, and language courses shall be placed under the organizing rubric of Civic Philosophy. The change in terminology is intended to highlight a revalued and reconceived humanities education, one that would, among other things, work to recover what Ramin Jahanbegloo calls the "public task" of philosophy.[6] This means that "doing" philosophy cannot occur in ivory tower isolation, but rather must be brought down to the streets, as it were, in Socratic fashion. The moral foundation of this education would be anchored in the spirit of questioning, and would represent a creative update to the enlightenment impulse within the Western intellectual tradition. First the *imaginative*, and then the *institutional* refounding of this philosophical value, would mark a radical recovery of the human capacity for questioning.

Within this alternative paradigm of education, a new *philosophical* emphasis on the spirit of questioning is to be coupled with a new *civic* emphasis on developing a sense of participatory readiness within the young. The highest aim of a Civic Philosophy curriculum would thus be to synthesize the development of individual human flourishing alongside the development of one's active civic engagement. In this manner, the pursuit of happiness is reconfigured to mean something much different from what it means today. Namely, that happiness and its pursuit, as an

---

[6] A concisely formulated moral justification for integrating the "public task" of philosophy into educational spheres can be found in, Ramin Jahanbegloo, "Preface." In *Gadflies in the Public Space: A Socratic Legacy of Philosophical Dissent*. Lanham: Rowman & Littlefield, 2017, xiii–xxvi.

unalienable right, should include the right of all Americans to have their civic capacities developed on an equal, non-discriminatory basis. Because unequal forms of civic education create not merely unequal citizens but also citizens that have become non-citizens in a moral sense, it would be warranted to begin reinterpreting the *pursuit* of happiness in light of current school equity litigation (such as we see implicit in the *Cook v. Raimondo* case).

In contrast to the prevailing conception of education rooted in depositing facts and information into the minds of students, aided and abetted by a culture of high-stakes testing, a Civic Philosophy curriculum would aim instead to shift our teacher's chief focus to what Neil Postman has called "the art and science of asking questions":

> But let us suppose, as Jefferson did and, much later, John Dewey, that a democratic society must take the risk, that such a society will be improved by citizens of a critical mind, and that the best way for citizens to protect their liberty is for them to be encouraged to be skeptical, to be suspicious of authority, and to be prepared (and unafraid) to resist propaganda.[7]

Postman's primary recommendation deserves extended quotation:

> The first suggestion is not controversial but is nonetheless the least likely to be taken seriously. I refer to the possibility that we would actually teach children something about the art and science of asking questions. No one, I assume, would deny that all knowledge we have is a result of our asking questions; indeed, that question-asking is the most significant intellectual tool that human beings have. Is it not curious, then, that the most significant intellectual skill available to human beings is not taught in school? ...Such learning is at the heart of reasoning and its product, skepticism. Do we dare do such a thing? Have you heard anyone talk about this? The president, the secretary of education, a school superintendent? They want our students to be answer-givers, not question-askers.[8]

Postman wrote these words twenty years ago, at about the same time the neoliberal educational reform movement was launching its answer-driven regime of high-stakes testing. His philosophically friendly proposal stands as a scathing and cogent indictment of today's impoverished

---

[7] Neil Postman, "Education." In *Building a Bridge to the 18th Century: How the Past Can Improve Our Future.* New York: Alfred Knopf, 1999, 160.

[8] Ibid., 162.

conception of educational purpose. More constructively, Postman's proposal stands as a moral and conceptual foundation for imagining a new,
Jeffersonian-inspired reconstruction of educational purpose.

On this foundation, then, one of the practical classroom applications of
such an approach shall include, but not be limited to, a renewed emphasis
on asking questions about the idea and meaning of America itself. Asking
questions about the meaning of the idea of America represents something
of a national tradition. Cornel West makes a persuasive case that American
pragmatism, at its best, captures this tradition's questioning spirit. For
West, American pragmatism reflects

> A conception of philosophy as a form of cultural criticism in which the
> meaning of America is put forward by intellectuals in response to dis-
> tinct social and cultural crises. American pragmatism is less a philosophical
> tradition putting forward solutions to perennial problems in the Western
> philosophical conversation initiated by Plato and more a continuous cul-
> tural commentary or set of interpretations that attempt to explain America
> to itself at a particular historical moment.[9]

By undertaking the pedagogical enterprise of "explaining America to
itself at this historical moment," we mean that teachers would be encouraged in their classrooms, with students, to form inquiries into the defining moral controversies of American society. In other words, rather than
systematically ignoring that which divides and unites the country, as civi-
cally bereft curriculums generally do today, a Civic Philosophy curriculum
would encourage students in their attempts, as Dewey had hoped, for
American citizens "to know conditions as they are."[10] Such an approach
will immediately give rise to messy conflicts over competing truth claims,
and this is largely the point. For these conflicts represent educationally fertile moral spaces—as such, they would seem to represent the experiential
nucleus of civic education. Under the rubric of a Civic Philosophy curricular approach, such moral predicaments can be framed and welcomed
as constituting so many sites of debate and negotiation, hopefully giving

---

[9] Cornel West, *The American Evasion of Philosophy: A Genealogy of Pragmatism*. Madison: University of Wisconsin Press, 1989, 5.

[10] John Dewey, "Creative Democracy—The Task Before Us." In *The Essential Dewey:
Volume 1: Pragmatism, Education, Democracy*, eds. Larry A. Hickman and Thomas M.
Alexander. Bloomington, IN: Indiana University Press, 1998, 343.

rise to the formation of new inquiries, new desires to know, and eventually new opinions. Unlike today's curriculum that has largely banished treatment of controversial issues, a Civic Philosophy curriculum is designed to create spaces for students to at least have the possibility of learning the skill and value of dialoguing across difference, a key democratic personality trait. Thus, critical inquiry into the idea of America should not be seen simply as a problem to be avoided, but rather, it must come to be seen as a magnificent problem that holds vast educational potential.

Although Jefferson is seldom mentioned as a prominent figure within the tradition of American pragmatism, there's good reason to frame his revolutionary theory as one of its philosophical precursors.[11] In order to briefly unpack this crucial affinity, let us recall an axiom of Jefferson's revolutionary theory. That is, the idea that the capacity to revise at both the individual and cultural level is paramount. Without this revisionary capacity being properly cultivated and drawn out, as outlined in Chapter 3, transitions toward democracy and transitions toward better conceptions of truth, simply couldn't occur. Similarly, when American pragmatists frame "truth" as a provisional or revisable quality, they do so because of a prior assumption that historical conditions inevitably change; thus, as conditions change, as human needs change, and as the march of generations proceed, it follows that conceptions of truth ought to change. If this assertion signifies a core foundational principle of American pragmatism—as I contend that it does in a general sense—we are positioned to acknowledge that Jefferson's processual interpretation of both democratic transition and Nature herself, qualifies his revolutionary thought as an intellectual source of this defining element of American pragmatism. In any case, the larger point is for teachers to imagine the myriad ways in which this crucial democratic tradition could be usefully applied within an emerging Civic Philosophy curriculum.

One way to meet this challenge, as earlier chapters have suggested, is to begin treating—virtually for the first time—the Declaration of Independence as a foundational text of the Civic Philosophy curriculum. To begin with, rather than requiring American middle school students to take a high-stakes "Constitution Test" in order to graduate to the next

---

[11] Ibid., 216. It is worth noting that West in no way ignores Jefferson's background contribution to the questing, reform minded strands of American pragmatism. He deftly links Jefferson and Rousseau to a romantic strain that reflects a "conception of imagination as a human power that conceives of social reality from a vantage point of change and for the purposes of transformation." This is a useful way to conceive of how Jefferson's revolutionary thought is so intimately tied to the formation of his broader educational purposes.

grade, the new mandate for all American students—at the elementary, middle, and high school levels—will be for them to write essays about the relationship between the Declaration of Independence and the Constitution. Specifically, by examining the *interactive dynamic* that connects the nation's two birth certificates, students will gain an appreciation for how the *moral values* of American political culture, as expressed in the Declaration (notably the equality, pursuit of happiness, and alter and abolish clauses), have interacted historically with the *legal framework* which is the Constitution.

Once again, as was said in previous chapters, we can safely conjecture that Jefferson would applaud Lincoln's effort to elevate the importance of the Declaration's moral values (the "apple of gold") above the legal structures of the Constitution (the "picture of silver"). Indeed, both the occasional clashes and occasional harmonies that have existed between the Declaration and the Constitution could be tracked by students and adopted as theoretical-scaffoldings for better understanding the frequently baffling trajectories of US political history. At the very least, such a nationally mandated essay test—in addition to the novel inquiries that it would spark—would prove infinitely more conducive, for example, to the creation of individuals who know and feel what participatory readiness means within the American political tradition. Such an exercise would undoubtedly serve higher democratic civic ends than our present policy of requiring students to memorize the structure of the Constitution, particularly when that structure is all too often "learned" as something drained of moral substance. The two approaches I am contrasting here illustrate the momentous distinction between learning *about* democratic procedures, on the one hand, and learning *to be* democratic on the other. It makes no sense to encourage students to memorize the Constitution's silver legal structure while encouraging them to ignore the Declaration's gold moral values. What makes "the Constitution test" a particularly misguided curricular policy, then, is that its institutionalization can easily have the effect of "de-moralizing" our student's *experience* of civic education within the schools.

The emerging paradigm shift in education that the K-12 Curricular Redesign envisions must also take seriously the goal of implementing an interdisciplinary reintegration. That is why, within the domain of Civic Philosophy, the conventionally separate disciplines of History/Government/Social Studies and that of English/Literature/Writing are placed under the same organizing banner. While the two branches of learning have different thematic foci, both areas of study are inseparable from a broader normative standpoint. Their normative inseparability lies in the fact that each is concerned with cultivating the capacities of students to read, to write, to think, and to speak, all for the purpose of acting in their lives both individually and collaboratively with a more wholesome discretion. In this way, combining the two disciplinary traditions not just rhetorically but in actuality promises to magnify the powers of each tradition.

In her trenchant analyses, Martha Nussbaum spotlights the destructive consequences of gutting the arts and humanities from the nation's curriculum.[12] Nussbaum outlines the ways in which these curricular trends harm America's fragile democratic culture. Nussbaum demonstrates the various ways in which the arts and humanities can be recruited to radically unsettle both the vertical model of the Self/Other difference as well as culturally learned forms of ignorance. The future of American democracy rests in no small measure on the manner in which Americans learn to "see" Otherness as well as our own forms of ignorance—and clearly the two are connected.

Nussbaum repeatedly emphasizes that the economic imperatives sequestered within what we have called the neoliberal paradigm of education has resulted in a regrettable "forgetting about the soul." Quite aware of the religious and delicate connotations of the term soul, Nussbaum posits an alternative secular definition whose discursive recovery, she believes, would tend to create healthier emotional climates within the schools.

> We seem to be forgetting about the soul, about what it is for thought to open out of the soul and connect person to world in a rich, subtle, and complicated manner; about what it is to approach another person as a soul, rather than as a mere useful instrument or an obstacle to one's own plans; about what it is to talk to someone who has a soul to someone else whom one sees as similarly deep and complex.[13]

The corollary to Nussbaum's proposition, of course, is that when schools and teachers operate without a soul-oriented discourse, it tends to produce emotionally barren, anti-erotic educational climates, climates that

---

[12] Martha Nussbaum, *Not for Profit: Why Democracy Needs the Humanities*. Princeton: Princeton University Press, 2010.

[13] Ibid., 6.

nicely compliment a culture of high-stakes testing. By advocating for a recovery of the term soul as an educational heuristic, Nussbaum wants educators, whether or not they accept this terminology in a formal sense, to appreciate at least the rich meanings that lie beneath its linguistic surface. She defines soul awareness as

> The faculties of thought and imagination that make us human and make our relationships rich human relationships, rather than relationships of mere use and manipulation. When we meet in society, if we have not learned to see both self and other in that way, imagining in one another inner faculties of thought and emotion, democracy is bound to fail, because democracy is built upon respect and concern, and these in turn are built upon the ability to see other people as human beings, not simply as objects.[14]

In Nussbaum's elegant formulations, literature, art, music, and dance emerge as the necessary curricular corollaries of a soul-oriented education. It is the curricular tradition of the humanities, in other words, that can best cultivate the human capacity for imagination and for self-revision, qualities that enable us to empathize and dignify the souls of others.

Another educational antidote to current antidemocratic trends would be for the schools to revalue the importance of literature. Nussbaum acknowledges that not all literature is democratic friendly and capable of promoting the moral ends that she has in mind. To return to the Civic Philosophy project of unsettling the vertical model of the self/other difference, Nussbaum argues that certain forms of literature encourage readers to both identify a particular culture's "blind-spots" while also "cultivating their inner-eyes."[15] These two ontological conditions—recognizing one's cultural blind-spots and cultivating of one's inner eyes—represent potential experiential outcomes of an education willing to promote the democratic value of relating to one another as equals, as dignified, as having inner depth and worth.

To summarize, the Civic Philosophy curricular reorganization responds to the urgent need to reintroduce civic education into the schools in a robust, interdisciplinary manner. The emphasis on questioning throughout the curriculum is significant, for the capacity to question must first

[14] Ibid., 6.
[15] Ibid., 108.

be exercised and cultivated if we are to activate our students' capacities for revision and hopefulness. Indeed, the act of questioning precedes and enables the human capacity to revise and to hope, which, as Chapter 3 argues, symbolizes the experiential guts of Jefferson's revolutionary theory. Only with a new emphasis on a culture of questioning can the public schools respond to the civic needs of our youth—and only then can the schools play their necessary role in transforming American identity into a more democratic version of itself.

Ecological Studies (the Need for Ecological Awareness)

A glance at the historical record demonstrates that the American people have slowly but surely shown a capacity to revise their political, cultural, and educational forms when the growing need to do so proved impossible to ignore. Yet, the challenge now, as always, is different: Can the nation enact this same capacity for revision in relation to the need to respond intelligently to the climate catastrophes we are witnessing, catastrophes that will surely intensify in the coming decades? And will the schools, for their part, respond forthrightly to the climate crisis through bold curricular renovation, or will they continue to impose upon students forms of structural ignorance in relation to global warming?

In order to respond intelligently to the problem of global warming, it seems evident that America's capacity to revise will need to be, once again, fully mobilized. Among other things, the challenge of global warming appears to call forth this very human capacity: a calling forth which could be called "revision for the sake of survival." For without the mobilization of our capacities to revise now, especially given the COVID-19 challenges, prospects for a decent future, or for any future, dim considerably. What is stake, then, isn't only the nation's ability or inability to change its course peacefully through the deliberation of complicated policy issues, although this process is clearly important. What is at stake, ultimately, is our identity as a democratic republic. Because this fragile symbol system (our imagined national identity), relies on revision to renew itself and change things for the better, if the American republic fails to summon up this power of revision as a means of survival, it will die. A democratic republic therefore must learn to rethink how to respond to the environmental crisis that we humans have, in profound ways, created for ourselves. For this reason, in the decades ahead, in line with creatively extending America's best political traditions, our public school curriculums must evidence, as part of their new mandate, a bold new receptivity to the revision of educational purpose.

Of course, there are excellent environmental education programs in place today across the country. However, generally speaking, such programs are all too rare and thus not in a position to shape the attitudes of a critical mass of young people. What we need is an updated and radically expanded version of environmental education, a curricular renovation that could be effectuated under the rubric of Ecological Studies. To situate this proposal in a national context, an Ecological Studies curriculum could be regarded as the progressive educational component of a Green New Deal.[16] Under such legislation, for example, federal resources would be deployed for the purpose of promoting ecological literacy in every public school in the nation. While some may balk at the prospect of recruiting Jefferson as an ally in this project of curricular repurposing, there's ample evidence to suggest that, were he around today, Jefferson would strongly endorse the scientific, ethical, and educational aims of an Ecological Studies curriculum. In the pages ahead, I make the case that Jefferson's brilliant yet largely overlooked writings on climate furnish a solid moral foundation for justifying an invigorated Ecological Studies curriculum.

JEFFERSON AS THE FIRST GREEN PRESIDENT

Probably few Americans today are aware of the fact that Jefferson was an avid meteorologist and climate scientist, having compiled copious daily notes on various weather patterns in Virginia over a period of five decades.[17] Indeed, few of us are aware that Jefferson was one of the first Americans to obtain a thermometer, having purchased it from an importer in Philadelphia just days before the Declaration was publicly released. This

---

[16] For a sympathetic interpretation of the Green New Deal, see Naomi Klein, *On Fire: The (Burning) Case For a Green New Deal.* New York: Simon & Schuster, 2018.

[17] This section of the chapter is grounded largely but not exclusively in the following four texts. Thomas Jefferson, "Query VII on Climate." In *Notes on the State of Virginia.* New York: Literary Classics of the United States, 1984, 200–208; Edwin T. Martin, "Meteorology." In *Thomas Jefferson: Scientist.* New York: Harry Schuman, 1952, 131–147; Silvio A. Bedini, *Thomas Jefferson: Statesman of Science.* New York: Macmillan, 1990; Keith Thomson, "Climate and Geography." In *Jefferson's Shadow: The Story of His Science.* New Haven: Yale University Press, 2012, 179–194.

purchase allowed Jefferson to report that, on July 4, 1776, the temperature was a pleasant 76 degrees Fahrenheit in Philadelphia![18] While these curious facts might seem inconsequential, they are nevertheless worth noting because they underscore one very consequential fact: That Jefferson loved to study the weather. Jefferson turned his inquisitive mind toward developing the science of meteorology not only because it was pleasurable for him to do so. More importantly, he was convinced that its study would reap practical benefits for the new nation. As Silvio A. Bedini writes:

> Jefferson continued to be concerned about weather observations on a national scale. For him it was not merely a hobby nor just a matter of scientific curiosity. He was aware that climatic conditions and the manner in which they varied from one part of the country to another were of considerable importance and affected the progress of the American population and the cultivation of a variety of plants and crops...Early in his career, even before the American Revolution, he had visualized the institution of a weather service on a national scale. The slow advancement of the science of meteorology distressed him, and he continued to hope that some means of recording observations with exactitude could be developed in each of the states.[19]

From this passage, we can infer that Jefferson strongly believed in the science of meteorology and thought that it had an important role to play in producing new knowledge about the earth's atmospheric conditions and climate. Bedini notes that Jefferson was "distressed" about the slow advancement of meteorology. No doubt, this distress signaled that Jefferson understood that further delay in promoting meteorology would mean that Americans could not avail themselves of the new discoveries and truths that the nascent discipline would have surely produced.

From our contemporary perch, we can only wonder what Jefferson would say today in reply to President Trump's oft-repeated opinion that global warming is a "hoax." We can only wonder how Jefferson would regard the climate change "debates" occurring today, to say nothing of the strange discourses swirling about the COVID-19 pandemic. Debates in which media pundits seem to share the same moral authority

---

[18] Thomson, 179–180.

[19] Bedini, 457.

as members of the international scientific community. From an educational policy standpoint, let us conjecture what positions Jefferson might adapt in relation to the moral and political predicament of global warming. Would Jefferson's twenty-first-century curriculum, for example, seek to promote the aims of climate science and ecological awareness? Needless to say, when we ask questions about what Jefferson might think or do in any given situation today, we engage in a form of thought experiment. We construct a set of Jeffersonian standards in our imagination, and use them as criterion of judgment for interpreting important features of today's political, cultural, and educational landscape. It must be noted, however, that no one has to wonder today what Jefferson's thoughts were about whether human activity can have an impact on the climate. Jefferson wrote that human culture and activity had already shaped climate patterns in his day—a stance that has important contemporary implications. This is the case because those who deny the scientific basis of global warming, tend also to deny that human activity is even capable of effecting something as vast as the earth's atmosphere and weather. Jefferson begs to differ.

In both his *Notes on the State of Virginia* and in a long letter to French physicist Jean Baptiste Le Roy (1786), Jefferson speculated that practices of deforestation in Virginia (called "clearing" at the time) exercised a noticeable effect on that region's climate.[20] In addition, toward the end of his life, in an 1824 letter to a meteorologist colleague, Jefferson reaffirms his strong belief in the science of meteorology as well as his belief that human activity creates climate change.

I thank you, sir, for your pamphlet on the climate of the West, and have read it with great satisfaction. Although it does not yet establish a satisfactory theory, it is an additional step towards it. Mine was perhaps the first attempt, not to form a theory, but to bring together the few facts then known and suggest them to public attention. They were written between 40 & 50 years ago, before the close of the revolutionary war, when the Western country was a wilderness untrodden but by the foot of the savage or the hunter. It is now flourishing in population and science, and after a few years more of observation and collection of facts will doubtless furnish a theory of solid foundation. Years are requisite for this, steady attention

---

[20] For anyone who doubts the brilliance of Jefferson's interpretations of climate, I would suggest they read his long dissertation-like letter to Jean Baptiste Le Roy. November 13, 1786. Founders Online, National Archives. https://founders.archives.gov/documents/Jefferson/01/10-02-0381.

to the thermometer, to the plants growing there, the times of their leafing & flowering, its animal inhabitants, beasts, birds, reptiles & insects, it's prevalent winds, quantities of rain and snow, temperature of fountains and other indexes of climate. We want this indeed for all the states, and the work should be repeated once or twice in a century to *shew the effect of clearing and culture towards changes of climate*.[21] (my emphasis)

Jefferson thus took to his grave the conviction that "the effects of clearing and culture" were key variables in producing climate change. For Jefferson, then, and notably for Benjamin Franklin, the prevailing common sense among meteorologists at that time was that human activity was in fact changing weather conditions in North America in the 1780s.[22]

In considering debates about whether or not human activity is responsible for global warming, young Americans, in particular, would benefit by recognizing that Jefferson and Franklin (along with many of their contemporaries) believed that human activity and civilizational development itself, was fully capable of producing changes in climate. And to their credit, both founders arrived at this conclusion before the Industrial Revolution accelerated and began wreaking its havoc on the global climate system.

The more we learn about Jefferson's passionate study of the earth's climate, the more we are persuaded that he would absolutely be receptive to the formation of a robust Ecological Studies curriculum. Such a curricula would include, as one of its core aims, the acquisition of climate-oriented knowledge and how this interacts with other fields of inquiry. As Thomson's work shows, Jefferson's writings on climate highlight his scientific interest in the intersections of climate, geography, nature, and agriculture.[23] The Ecological Studies curriculum is envisioned to engage these intersections as well.

To help actualize these curricular renovations, monies extracted from the federal government's war budget, augmented by assets appropriated from its military landholdings, could be redirected to the schools to aid in the study of climate change, an issue which can now be framed as a

---

[21] Thomas Jefferson to Lewis E. Beck, July 16, 1824. https://founders.archives.gov/documents/Jefferson/98-01-02-4410.

[22] Thomson, 188.

[23] Ibid., 193.

national security concern.[24] The goal will be to encourage all American children to become ecologically literate. The definition of "ecologically literate" will include the development of a familiarity with the facts and knowledge pertaining to climate science. However, just as importantly, the definition of ecological literacy must also include the development of certain ethical capacities, in such a manner that would encourage the young to be willing and able to act on behalf of their raised ecological awareness. To borrow from Allen's civic moral ideal once again, this ethical dimension of the curriculum would be designed to enhance a sense of "participatory readiness" within the young, which would enable them to act on behalf of the social, cultural, and political problem of climate change. Within the Ecological Studies curriculum, it shall be deemed insufficient for students to merely accumulate knowledge about the pertinent facts of climate change and the science that underlies it, if that crucial knowledge is not accompanied by an equally crucial willingness to act on its behalf.[25] In addition, the essential ethical component of this curricular repurposing finds moral anchorage in all three of the moral propositions discussed in previous chapters: *the earth belongs to the living*, the *pursuit of happiness* and the *alter and abolish* clauses.

Finally, as another component of this curricular renovation, action must be taken so that a million well-resourced gardens will bloom and flourish in every K-12 public school in America. The size and nature of these gardens (indoor or outdoor) will vary according to geography, but also according to demographic need, similar to how the size of gymnasiums vary from elementary schools to high schools. The gardens could provide healthy, vegetable, and fruit-based sources of food for every child in the country, a practical benefit that's needed now more than ever.[26]

[24] For a stunning account of the Pentagon's treatment of global warming as a national security issue, see Michael T. Klare, *All Hell Breaking Loose: The Pentagon's Perspective on Climate Change*. New York: Metropolitan Books, 2019.

[25] The "ethical action" dimension of an Ecological Studies curriculum that I discuss, is also prominently featured in the "competencies, knowledge and dispositions" section of the Executive Summary of the North American Association for Environmental Education (NAAEE).

[26] Compare this vision to the "vision" of the Trump administration, which recently announced substantial federal cuts to school lunch funding: "Nearly 1 million low-income students would lose automatic access to free school lunches under a proposal from President Donald Trump's administration that aims to limit the number of people receiving

Just as there are already some superb environmental education programs operating today, but not nearly enough, so, too, are there already superb school garden programs today, but not nearly enough. It used to be different: the USDA has estimated that, in 1906, there were 75,000 school gardens in the United States.[27] Here, then, is yet another American tradition that should undergo a renaissance.[28] For example, Ventura Unified School District in California has developed a nationally recognized model that links school gardening, nutrition education, and a farm-to-school lunch program featuring locally grown fruits and vegetables for 17,000 public school students.[29] In addition to providing healthy food and serving as models of good nutrition, the gardens would also serve as *primary classroom sites* for the newly organized science curriculum. This reform would bring the farm to the scientific table, as it were, whereby a range of traditional scientific inquiries, such as agriculture, botany, biology, horticulture, etc., could take place at the gardens with renewed practicality. In short, school garden programs would no longer operate episodically in an ad hoc fashion as they do now, but would be nationalized in scope, thus giving new meaning to the phrase "the greening of America."

CRITICAL MEDIA LITERACY (THE NEED TO DISTINGUISH BETWEEN TRUTH AND FALSITY)

Throughout these pages, we have seen that Jefferson believed deeply in the values of the Enlightenment. Residing at the core of Jefferson's enlightenment ethos was an article of faith, a faith in the capacity of ordinary people to govern themselves on the basis of reason and truth. Significantly, this faith included a faith in their capacity to revise their understandings of reality. It was this faith that caused Jefferson to make education and the transformation of the multitude the moral foundation of his

---

federal food stamps," *USA Today*, October 27, 2019. http://usatoday.com/story/new/education/2019/10/27/school-lunch-free-trump-foodstamps/2457920001/.

[27] UCfoodobserver.com/2015/05/06/a-history-of-school-gardens-and-how-the-model-is-getting-a-boost-today-from-food-corps.

[28] For a scholarly work on the origins of the school garden movement that Dewey greatly encouraged, see Sally Kohlstedt, "A Better Crop of Boys and Girls: The School Garden Movement, 1890–1920." *History of Education Quarterly*, Vol. 48, No. 1, 2008, 58–93.

[29] https://healthyventuracounty.org/healthy-schools/farm-to-school-gardens.

growth-oriented revolutionary theory. Jefferson understood that reason and truth were not only developmental and educable human capacities, they were also "contestable" and thus foundational to democratic citizenship. Considering his enlightenment outlook, Jefferson could be expected to lament the fact that Americans now seem to inhabit what many keen observers have dubbed a post-truth and post-fact cultural environment.[30] As Jefferson once again rolls in his grave, we might imagine him posing some tough questions for us: *What happened to the values of reason and truth as the moral basis of American identity? Are these ideals salvageable today? How might the schools respond to these trends?*

Remarkably enough, in the frenzied political atmosphere preceding his election to the presidency in 1800, Jefferson identified strikingly similar discordant cultural trends (albeit in embryonic form). To appreciate Jefferson's insights into what we might call, for want of a better term, the politics of truth, we turn to an 1804 letter he wrote to jurist and political supporter, John Tyler, regarding the 1800 campaign season:

> ...Amidst the direct falsehoods, the misrepresentations of truth, the calumnies & insults resorted to by a faction to mislead the public mind, & to overwhelm those intrusted with its interests, our support is to be found in the approving voice of our conscience and country, in the testimony of our fellow citizens that their confidence is not to be shaken by these artifices.[31]

Despite the vexed circumstances of his day, Jefferson still maintains his enlightenment faith in the capacity of the American people to resist the seductive lure of political propaganda—to avoid having their confidence "shaken by these artifices." Crucially in view of the book's civic aims, Jefferson proceeds in the Tyler letter to establish a foundational *moral correlation* between the fate of the nation's experiment in self-government and the American people's ability to act, as citizens, on the basis of reason and truth. Jefferson opines,

> No experiment can be more interesting than what we are now trying, & which we trust will end in establishing the fact that man may be governed

[30] Perhaps one of the finest accounts of this phenomenon is Michiko Kakutani's, *The Death of Truth: Notes on Falsehood in the Age of Trump*. New York: Tim Duggan Books, 2018.

[31] Thomas Jefferson to John Tyler, June 28, 1804. https://founders.archives.gov/documents/Jefferson/01-43-02-0557.

by reason and truth. Our first object should therefore be to leave open to him all avenues of truth, the most effectual hitherto found is the freedom of the press. It is therefore the first shut up by those who fear the investigation of their actions. The firmness with which the people have withstood the late abuses of the press, the discernment they have manifested between truth and falsehood, show that they may be safely trusted to hear everything true and false, & to form a correct judgment between them...I hold it therefore certain that to open the doors of truth, & to fortify the habit of testing everything by reason, are the most effectual manacles we can rivet on the hands of our successors to prevent their manacling the people with their own consent.[32]

Jefferson next moves to evaluate the "republican" character of the American people at the very moment their allegiance to republican principles was being severely tested. Jefferson soberly observes that they seemed to have abandoned their identification with republican principles:

...and their apparent readiness to abandon all the principles established for their protection seemed for a while to countenance the opinions of those who say they cannot be trusted with their own government. But I never doubted their rallying: & they did rally much sooner than I had expected, on the whole that experiment on their credulity has confirmed my confidence in their ultimate good sense and virtue.[33]

For Jefferson, then, a democratic republic must guard against those subtle and no so subtle authoritarian narratives that abandon fact in favor of fiction, reason in favor of emotion, and truth in favor of ignorance. Not to directly confront such trends, particularly within the schools, can only further erode the moral and institutional foundations that permit power relations and other political issues in a democratic society to be debated and contested in the first place. Because respect for the values of reason and truth are foundational to the formation of democratic citizenship, it would seem to follow from a Jeffersonian standpoint that the public schools should today refashion their curricular purposes in order to protect and actively develop these values, habits and capacities.

The 1804 letter to Tyler also tells us that Jefferson recognized the very real possibility that America's democratic experiment could unspool

[32] Ibid.
[33] Ibid.

itself, so to speak. Jefferson points out that, during the campaign of 1800, the American people were, in his words, "artfully thrown" into moral confusion by political factions bent on manipulating public opinion. As earlier chapters demonstrate, Jefferson regularly expressed concern that ambitious tyrants and their cunning machineries of disinformation might succeed in shaking the American people's confidence in the republican values and habits of mind.

Clearly, Jefferson was acutely aware of the moral and political zones of danger posed by the print media and the demagogues of his day. We have good reason to believe, moreover, that were Jefferson around today, he would be quick to recognize the totalizing and thus more ominous zones of danger posed by the digitally saturated world we inhabit today. Given what we know about Jefferson, it's no huge leap to suggest that he would recognize the need to transform the nation's curriculum so as to address these technological developments and novel historical circumstances. In short, Jefferson would want the young to be initiated into understanding the moral and political complexities of their ubiquitous media environment.

Instructively for our purposes, one critical media literacy scholar has recently framed Jefferson as a natural ally to this increasingly relevant academic discipline. According to Rob Williams:

> I imagine that Jefferson himself, were he alive today, would support this volume's focus on critical medial literacy, defined in these pages as an educational response that expands the notion of media literacy to include different forms of mass communication, popular culture, and new technologies, focusing on the ideology critique and analyzing the politics of representation of crucial dimensions of gender, race, class, and sexuality.[34]

Because the world of social media has become a central medium through which concepts of fact, truth, and reason are formed (and so much more), it is perfectly fitting for Williams to turn to the Jeffersonian tradition to underwrite the moral legitimacy of critical media studies. Amazingly in this regard, notice how Williams links Jefferson to the work of Umberto Eco, one of the world's foremost media critics.

---

[34] Rob Williams, "Fighting 'Fake News' in An Age of Digital Disinformation." In *Critical Media Literacy and Fake News in a Post-Truth America*, eds. Z. Christian Goering and Paul Thomas. Boston: Brill/Sense Books, 2018, 54.

As a U.S. media historian, I understand that the framers of the republic (Thomas Jefferson chief among them) believed that the only way the United States might survive as a democracy was if "virtuous" (meaning public spirited and civic minded) citizens developed capacities to critically read, write and think for themselves and in civic communities. As Italian semiotician Umberto Eco explained, channeling Jefferson on the eve of the digital age, "a democratic civilization will save itself only if it makes the language of the image into a stimulus for critical reflection—not an invitation to hypnosis."[35]

For Williams, then, Eco was "channeling Jefferson" in the sense that he identifies Jefferson with the axiom that democracy can only survive if its citizens learn to regard the "language of the image as a stimulus for critical reflection and not as an invitation to hypnosis." As we've seen, Jefferson's philosophy of education was designed to produce persons capable of making discriminating judgments between competing truth claims. This is precisely the kind of epistemological acumen that Jefferson believed was the ultimate moral guarantor of the republic's fragile existence. For these reasons and more, we affirm, with Williams, that Jefferson would recognize the need today to integrate a robust program of critical media literacy into a newly redesigned American curriculum.

It is, of course, obvious that our public schools are the primary institutions through which a curriculum for critical media literacy could be most effectively implemented. As suggested in the introductory section of the chapter, monies extracted from the federal government's war budget could be redirected to fund curricular programs that would initiate the young into thinking more deliberately about their media environment. The historical emergence and present ubiquity of social media has created a new need to understand not only its many perils, but also to understand its positive potential for democratic empowerment. The overarching purpose of a Critical Media Literacy approach, then, consistent with the growing literature on the subject, is to encourage the young to study their media environment not necessarily by removing them from inhabiting these spaces, but rather by promoting a sense of critical distance from, and study of, the overt and covert operations of these realms.

Appropriately enough, the University of Virginia (*UVA*), has recently undertaken a number of curricular initiatives—called Engagements—that

[35] Ibid., 54.

seek to address the lack of civic engagement among American youth.[36] Although the Engagements program focuses on higher education, the curricular renovations that *UVA* has put into practice have profound implications for K-12 education nationwide. In fact, the purposes of the Engagements initiative largely mirror the purposes of our K-12 Curricular Redesign. There are roughly ten courses in each of the four Engagement areas: Engaging Aesthetics, Empirical and Scientific Engagement, Engaging Differences, and Ethical Engagements. One course outline within the Ethical Engagements strand captures the spirit of what critical media literacy would look like in practice:

> Much research connects the use of digital media to problems with mental health and other forms of suffering. Acting on the premise that it is worth knowing whether this is true of ourselves, will explore the ethical implications of various dimensions of our digital media use. We will engage in a digital detox, or a break from all digital media, which students will process in writing and in dialogue with a small group of classmates. For our final project, students will work with their groups to co-author their best practices for using digital media and their ethical justifications of their best practices.[37]

If given the opportunity, it will not be difficult for creative teachers to experiment with how to assist the young as they learn how to judge, to choose, and to make distinctions in relation to their respective media environments. For example, in the spirit of Postman's question-based approach to education, a critical media pedagogy would ask, among other things, how to distinguish between genuine and fake news? What constitutes a legitimate source of news as opposed to an illegitimate source? What is an "algorithm" and how do they work?

For civic educators interested in fleshing-out the pedagogical implications of an invigorated critical media studies, Jaron Lanier's recent book, *Ten Arguments for Deleting Your Social Media Accounts Right Now* (2018) should be regarded as foundational.[38] As a technological pioneer

---

[36] A further description of the Engagements initiative can be found @ as.virginia.edu/engagements.

[37] Ibid.

[38] Jaron Lanier, *Ten Arguments for Quitting Your Social Media Accounts Right Now*. New York: Tim Duggan Books, 2018.

in Silicon Valley in the 1980s, Lanier occupies a unique position both as a computer scientist and as a philosopher of the digital age. Lanier is intimately familiar with the ways in which algorithms have been constructed not to serve the ends of democracy or human flourishing, but rather to serve the cause of profit for the benefit of "anonymous oligarchs."[39] Lanier argues that the current business model of social media represents a distortion of its original vision, and argues that there is no inherent reason why social media platforms have to operate in this manner. Notably for our purposes, Lanier shows how today's social media *undermines truth, destroys capacities for empathy,* and tends inexorably to make those who participate within its realms, *unhappy.* In short, Lanier's manifesto urges young Americans in particular to become cognizant of the political, psychological, and ethical intricacies of the new social media, for nothing less than their autonomy and freedom as persons is at stake.

Finally, to underscore the interdisciplinary character of Critical Media Education, students will be encouraged not only to analyze various media platforms and to explore various forms of media production, but also, allied art education courses will encourage students to focus on deciphering the signs, symbols, and aesthetics of our contemporary "visual culture." According to its leading practitioners, such as Kerry Freedman,[40] art education should focus much less attention, for example, on studying past artistic traditions and instead focus more attention on challenging students to interpret the vast field of educationally fertile symbols, signs, and aesthetics which constitute their contemporary visual environments. In this way, the newly constituted art curriculum would turn around from a traditional focus on the past, toward a new focus on the present—making the Spectacle itself an object of critical reflection rather than an invitation to hypnosis.

[39] Ibid., 3–5.

[40] Kerry Freedman, "Curriculum as Process: Visual Culture and Democratic Education." In *Teaching Visual Culture: Curriculum, Aesthetics and the Social Life of Art.* New York: Teachers College Press, 2003, 106–127.

Post-script: America's Once
and Future Revolution

In almost every chapter of the book, we have seen various ways in which Jefferson's revolutionary theory was the product of a unique eighteenth-century context. In Part I, the primary objective was to anchor Jefferson's theory in its historical particularity. However, in Parts II and III, experimental efforts were undertaken to interpret Jefferson's theory as that which also contains a recoverable republican moral spirit. This paradigmatic model was used not only as a tool of critical analysis to illuminate both present and future, but also as a moral compass to point us in new curricular directions. Owing to the fact that I theorized Jefferson's revolutionary thought according to the three-part structure of a jeremiad, the present and future implications of Jefferson's theory were accentuated to identify and condemn present-day anti-republican trends and practices. I adopted the jeremiad's thematic sequence of promise, declension, and renewal in the first place, because this rhetorical tradition seemed to perfectly match the genesis and trajectory of Jefferson's revolutionary theory.

As the book nears its completion, it bears repeating that Jefferson's revolutionary theory can assist reformers today who wish to establish a moral foundation for reconstructing educational purpose beyond the narrow "econometrics" of the neoliberal paradigm.

I have further suggested that the three pillars of Jefferson's revolutionary theory—*the earth belongs to the living*, the *pursuit of happiness*, and the *alter and abolish* clause—each in their own way, but also cumulatively, represent potentially powerful instruments of civic engagement and action. As I have tried to demonstrate, these three moral propositions can be recruited pedagogically to expose the anomalies and contradictions rapidly accumulating within the neoliberal paradigm of education. And, just as Danielle Allen urges us to read the text of the Declaration as a critical heuristic of the present, I am persuaded that they can and should be similarly framed as critical heuristics of Jefferson's future-directed revolutionary theory. Taken together, they give Americans license to throw off all of those inherited institutional and psychological shackles that suppress our democratic potential. The symbolic recovery of these magnificent moral propositions may well turn out to be a vital tipping point in our struggle to reverse and transcend the increasingly oligarchic and authoritarian trends that continue to threaten democratic life in America.

In reclaiming the value of Jefferson's revolutionary moral spirit for purposes of democratic transition—in both our education and politics—we should recognize that such a recovery would also be tantamount to reclaiming the best of the enlightenment tradition as a new cultural force in the enactment of America's next democratic revolution. Let us honor and care for this tradition by criticizing it as a means for its progressive renewal—just as Jefferson hoped we would.

References

Addis, C. 2003. *Jefferson's Vision for Education, 1760–1845*. New York: Peter Lang Books.

Allen, D. 2014. *Our Declaration: A Reading of the Declaration of Independence in Defense of Equality*. New York: W. W. Norton.

———. 2016. "What Is Education For?" *Boston Review*. May Issue.

Antczak, F. 1985. "Education in Thought and Character: The Rhetorical Reconstitution of Democracy." In *Thought and Character: The Rhetoric of Democratic Education*. Ames: Iowa State University Press, 197–205.

Ayers, W. 2019. "I Shall Create!" In *Teaching When the World Is On Fire*, ed. Lisa Delpit. New York: The New Press, 3–15.

Barber, B. 1998. "Thomas Jefferson and the Education of the Citizen." In *A Passion for Democracy*. Princeton: Princeton University Press, 161–177.

Bedini, S. 1990. *Thomas Jefferson: Statesman of Science*. New York: Macmillan Publishing.

Bernstein, R. J. 2018. "The American Revolution and the Revolutionary Spirit." In *Why Read Hannah Arendt Now*. Medford, MA: Polity Press, 103–116.

Bowles, J. and Hall, R., eds. 2010. *Seeing Jefferson Anew: In His Time and Ours*. Charlottesville: University of Virginia Press.

Brann, E. H. 1979. *Paradoxes of Education in a Republic*. Chicago: University of Chicago Press.

Bronner, S. 2004. *Reclaiming the Enlightenment: Toward a Politics of Radical Engagement*. New York: Columbia University Press.

Brown, W. 2015. *Undoing the Demos: Neoliberalism's Stealth Revolution*. Brooklyn, NY: Zone Books.

© The Editor(s) (if applicable) and The Author(s), under exclusive license to Springer Nature Switzerland AG, part of Springer Nature 2020
K. T. Burch, *Jefferson's Revolutionary Theory and the Reconstruction of Educational Purpose*, The Cultural and Social Foundations of Education, https://doi.org/10.1007/978-3-030-45763-1

Conant, J. 1963. *Thomas Jefferson and the Development of American Public Education*. Berkeley: University of California Press.

Counts, G. 1933. *A Call to the Teachers of the Nation*. New York: John Day Company.

———. 1938. *Prospects of American Democracy*. New York: John Day Company.

Delbanco, A. 1999. *The Real American Dream: A Meditation on Hope*. Cambridge: Harvard University Press.

Dewey, J. 1939/1989. "Democracy and America." In *Freedom and Culture*. New York: Prometheus Books, 119–134.

———, ed. 1940. *The Living Thoughts of Thomas Jefferson*. New York: Longman's Green and Comapny.

Ehrenberg, J. 1999. "Civil Society and Democratic Politics." In *Civil Society: The Critical History of an Idea*. New York: New York University Press, 233–250.

Engels, J. 2014. "Dewey on Jefferson: Reiterating Democratic Faith in Times of War." In *Trained Capacities: John Dewey, Rhetoric, and Democratic Practice*, eds. Brian Jackson and Gregory Clark. Columbia: University of South Carolina Press, 88–89.

Goering, C. and Thomas, P. 2018. *Critical Media Literacy and Fake News in Post-truth America*. Boston: Brill Sense.

Goetzman, William H. 2009. *Beyond the Revolution: A History of American Thought from Paine to Pragmatism*. New York: Basic Books.

Gutek, G. 1984. *George S. Counts and American Civilization: The Educator as Theorist*. Macon: Mercer University Press.

Gutzman, K. 2017. *Thomas Jefferson, Revolutionary: A Radical's Struggle to Remake America*. New York: St. Martin's Press.

Hardt, M. 2007. *Thomas Jefferson: The Declaration of Independence*. London: Verso Books.

Hellenbrand, H. 1990. *The Unfinished Revolution: Education and Politics in the Thought of Thomas Jefferson*. Newark: University of Delaware Press.

Hendriksen, T. 1990. *Empire of Liberty: The Statecraft of Thomas Jefferson*. New York: Oxford University Press.

Holowchak, M. 2014. *Thomas Jefferson's Philosophy of Education: A Utopian Dream*. New York: Routledge.

——— and Dotts, B., eds. 2017. *The Elusive Thomas Jefferson: Essays on the Man Behind the Myth*. Jefferson, NC: McFarland & Company.

Honeywell, R. 1931. *The Educational Work of Thomas Jefferson*. Cambridge: Harvard University Press.

Israel, J. 2017. *The Expanding Blaze: How the American Revolution Ignited the World, 1775–1848*. Princeton: Princeton University Press.

Jahanbegloo, R. 2017. *Gadflies in the Public Space: A Socratic Legacy of Philosophical Dissent*. Lanham: Lexington Books.

Jefferson, T. 1821/2005. *Autobiography of Thomas Jefferson*. Mineola, NY: Dover Books.
———. 1926/1974. *The Commonplace Book of Thomas Jefferson*. Baltimore, MD: Johns Hopkins University Press,
———. 1984. *Thomas Jefferson: Writings*. New York: Literary Classics of the United States.
Justice, B., ed. 2013. *The Founding Fathers, Education, and the Great Contest: The American Philosophical Society Prize of 1797*. New York: Palgrave Macmillan.
Kahn, R. 2010. *Critical Pedagogy, Ecoliteracy, & Planetary Crisis: The Ecopedagogy Movement*. New York: Peter Lang.
Kakutani, M. 2018. *The Death of Truth: Notes on Falsehood in the Age of Trump*. New York: Tim Duggan Books.
Kammen, M. 1978. *A Season of Youth: The American Revolution and the Historical Imagination*. New York: Oxford University Press.
Kellner, D. and Share, J. 2019. "Preparing Educators to Teach Critical Media Literacy." In *The Critical Media Literacy Guide: Engaging Media and Transforming Education*. Rotterdam, The Netherlands: Brill/Sense Publishers, 62–79.
Klare, M. 2019. *All Hell Breaking Loose: The Pentagon's Perspective on Climate Change*. New York: Metropolitan Books.
Klein, N. 2018. *On Fire: The (Burning) Case For a Green New Deal*. New York: Simon & Schuster.
Koch, A. 1943. *The Philosophy of Thomas Jefferson*. Chicago: Quadrangle Books.
Lanier, J. 2018. *Ten Arguments for Deleting Your Social Media Accounts Right Now*. New York: Henry Holt.
Lerner, R. 1987. *The Thinking Revolutionary: Principle and Practice in the New Republic*. Ithaca: Cornell University Press.
Loye, D. 2004. "Darwin's Lost Theory and the Hidden Crisis in Western Education." In *Education for a Culture of Peace*, eds. Rianne Eisler and Ron Miller. Portsmouth, NH: Heinemann, 42–55.
Lynd, S. 1968. *The Intellectual Origins of American Radicalism*. New York: Vintage Books.
Martin, E. 1952. *Thomas Jefferson: Scientist*. New York: Harry Schuman.
Matthews, R. 1984. *Thomas Jefferson: A Revisionist View*. Lawrence: University of Kansas Press.
McCoy, D. 1996. *The Elusive Republic: Political Economy in Jeffersonian America*. Chapel Hill: University of North Carolina Press.
McInnis, M. and Nelson, L. 2019. *Educated in Tyranny: Slavery and Thomas Jefferson's University*. Charlottesville: University of Virginia Press.
Murphy, Andrew R. 2009. *Prodigal Nation: Moral Decline and Divine Punishment From New England to 9/11*. New York: Oxford University Books.

Neem, J. 2017. *Democracy's Schools: The Rise of Public Education in America.* Baltimore: Johns Hopkins University Press.

Nussbaum, M. 2010. *Not for Profit: Why Democracy Needs the Humanities.* Princeton: Princeton University Press.

Ober, J. 1996. *The Athenian Revolution: Essays on Ancient Greek Democracy and Political Theory.* Princeton: Princeton University Press.

Pangle, L. and Pangle, T. 1993. *The Learning of Liberty: The Educational Ideals of the American Founders.* Lawrence: University of Kansas Press.

Patterson, C. 1967. *The Constitutional Principles of Thomas Jefferson.* Gloucester, MA: Peter Smith.

Peterson, M. 1960. *The Jefferson Image in the American Mind.* New York: Oxford University Press.

Postman, N. 1999. *Building a Bridge to the 18th Century: How the Past Can Improve Our Future.* New York: Alfred A. Knopf.

Ravitch, D. 2013. *Reign of Error: The Hoax of the Privatization Movement and the Danger to America's Public Schools.* New York: Alfred Knopf.

Richard, C. 2008. *Greeks and Romans Bearing Gifts: How the Ancients Inspired the Founding Fathers.* Lanham: Rowman & Littlefield.

Ryan, A. 1995. *John Dewey and the High Tide of American Liberalism.* New York: W. W. Norton.

Sarat, A., ed. 2005. *Dissent in Dangerous Times.* Ann Arbor: University of Michigan Press.

Schneirov, R. and Fernandez, G. 2014. *Democracy as a Way of Life in America: A History.* New York: Routledge.

Shelby, T. and Terry, B. 2018. *To Shape a New World: Essays on the Political Philosophy of Martin Luther King, Jr.* Cambridge: Harvard University Press.

Shiffren, S. 1999. *Dissent, Injustice, and the Meanings of America.* Princeton: Princeton University Press.

Shulman, G. 2008. *American Prophecy: Race and Redemption in American Political Culture.* Minneapolis: University of Minnesota Press.

Snowden, E. 2019. *Permanent Record.* New York: Metropolitan Books.

Snyder, T. 2017. *On Tyranny: Twenty Lessons From the Twentieth Century.* New York: Tim Duggan Books.

Staloff, D. 2005. *Hamilton, Adams and Jefferson: The Politics of Enlightenment and the American Founding.* New York: Hill and Wang.

Stitzlein, S. 2013. *Teaching For Dissent: Citizenship Education and Political Activism.* New York: Routledge Books.

Taylor, A. 2019. *Thomas Jefferson's Education.* New York: W. W. Norton.

Teachout, Z. 2014. *Corruption in America: From Benjamin Franklin's Snuff Box to Citizens United.* Cambridge: Harvard University Press.

Thomson, K. 2012. "Climate and Geography." In *Jefferson's Shadow: The Story of His Science.* New Haven: Yale University Press.

Traub, J. 2019. "Why Did One-Half of America Choose Illiberal Democracy." In *What Was Liberalism? The Past, Present and Promise of a Noble Idea.* New York: Basic Books, 243–255.

Wagoner, J. 2004. *Jefferson and Education.* Chapel Hill: University of North Carolina Press.

Watkins, W., ed. 2012. *The Assault on Public Education: Confronting the Politics of Corporate School Reform.* New York: Teachers College Press.

West, C. 1989. *The American Evasion of Philosophy: A Genealogy of Pragmatism.* Madison: University of Wisconsin Press.

Wolin, S. 2008. *Democracy, Inc.: Managed Democracy and the Specter of Inverted Totalitarianism.* Princeton: Princeton University Press.

Wood, G. 1989. *The Presence of the Past: Essays on the State and the Constitution.* Baltimore: Johns Hopkins University Press.

———. 1992. "What Revolutionary Action Means Today." In *Dimensions of Radical Democracy: Pluralism, Citizenship, Community,* ed. Chantal Mouffe. London: Verso, 249–256.

———. 1993. *The Radicalism of the American Revolution.* New York: Vintage Books.

Wulf, A. 2015. "Politics and Nature: Thomas Jefferson and Humboldt." In *The Invention of Nature: Alexander Von Humbolt's New World.* New York: Alfred A. Knopf, 94–108.

Yarbrough, J. 1998. *American Virtues: Thomas Jefferson on the Character of a Free People.* Lawrence: University of Kansas Press.

Index

CPSIA information can be obtained
at www.ICGtesting.com
Printed in the USA
LVHW031807040322
712646LV00009B/719